# Praise for *PheMOMenal Teacher*

*PheMOMenal Teacher* radiates honesty, care, and hope! Highly relatable, it's a lifeline for mom-teachers navigating life's complexities. Packed with practical wisdom, it's your go-to guide for finding that extra gear while acknowledging life's challenges and prioritizing self-care. With wholehearted vulnerability, Annick Rauch shares her experiences, offering invaluable insights to avoid burnout. She's fallen down and gotten back up, and in these pages, she generously shares her journey, so that others can find their own path to flourishing.

—**Lainie Rowell,** bestselling author, award-winning educator, and international keynote speaker

Annick shares her deeply personal journey with readers so we can learn to embrace our greatness as teaching moms with all of our fabulous flaws and often exhausting altruism. She shows us that loving ourselves first is essential to being able to love others limitlessly and that we really can shine bright without having to burn ourselves out. This book is right on time for those of us who want to give our all to the people we love the most—our families *and* our students—so we can live our best lives while helping them be able to do the very same. *PheMOMenal Teacher* will help you make your life even more MOMentous than it already is!

—**Dawn Harris,** mom, wife, educator, entrepreneur, and author of *Plan Like a Pirate*

Annick speaks from her heart, and her vulnerability and transparency are much needed for all mom-educators burning the candle at both ends. Readers are empowered to make themselves a priority and embrace the value and greatness within.

—**Traci Browder,** M.Ed., author, and speaker

PhenMOMenal Teacher is the heart-to-heart every educator mom didn't know they needed. Annick expertly weaves genuine experiences and life lessons with actionable strategies that provide hope, encouragement, and guidance for any mom in education. Her personal stories will resonate and warm your heart, helping you discover your strength and leaving you empowered to chase after your wildest dreams.

—**Tisha Richmond,** educator and author

Transform your struggles into strengths and be your best self. *PheMOMenal Teacher* is a must-read that reminds all moms and educators to carve out time from their calendar chaos to pursue their personal passions. You're worth this read!

—**Nycol Didcote,** second-grade French immersion teacher, M. Inclusive Ed.

Annick Rauch connects readers with their minds and hearts, sharing personal experiences that resonate far beyond the page. You will be inspired, uplifted, and encouraged to face day-to-day challenges while holding true to your purpose at home and at work. With relatable stories of struggles, achievements, and thoughtful reflections, this book will remind you of the three words that matter most: You. Are. Enough!

—**Tamara Letter,** M.Ed., instructional coach, technology integrator, and author of *A Passion for Kindness: Making the World a Better Place to Lead, Love, and Learn*

An absolute must-read for anyone looking to cultivate deep meaning, resilience, and self-care. Annick's writing is deeply moving and will speak to your heart. This book is a true gem, filled with heartfelt stories and invaluable insights to inspire and uplift you, leading you to be the best version of yourself. Rauch's emphasis on rest, community, and personal growth is refreshing and empowering. Her message of self-worth, gratitude, and taking small actions to make a significant impact will stay with you long after you finish reading and inspire and motivate you to chase your wildest dreams.

—**Elisabeth Bostwick,** founder of Inspire Innovation, educator, and author of *Take the L.E.A.P.: Ignite a Culture of Innovation*

Being an educator and being a mom are two of the hardest jobs in the world, but Annick Rauch's new book shows you how to gracefully integrate both roles into your daily life. She explains that self-care isn't selfish, she teaches us how to lean on others in the midst of our struggles, and she details the benefits of rest—even when it seems impossible.

As bonus, she includes reflection activities at the end of each chapter to help you apply her teacher mom wisdom. Although this book is written for women, as a dad and a teacher myself, I found incredible value within these pages.

—**Dan Tricarico,** author, *The Zen Teacher: Creating Focus, Simplicity, and Tranquility in the Classroom*

This enlightening read delves into the emotional rollercoaster of "mom guilt" and had me nodding throughout. Rauch's pragmatic advice and real-life anecdotes serve as a powerful testament to the fact that it is indeed possible to excel in your career while also being an attentive, nurturing parent and partner by giving yourself a little grace. This book is not just an essential guide for educators but a cornerstone for anyone aspiring to succeed both professionally and personally. Highly recommend!

—**Lynette White,** district and community relations coordinator

PheMOMenal Teacher

Pursue Your Dreams and Still
*Be Your Best Self* ♡
at Work and at Home

ANNICK RAUCH

*PheMOMenal Teacher: Pursue Your Dreams and Still Be Your Best Self at Work and at Home*
© 2023 Annick Rauch

All rights reserved. No part of this publication may be reproduced in any form or by any electronic or mechanical means, including information storage and retrieval systems, without permission in writing by the publisher, except by a reviewer who may quote brief passages in a review. For information regarding permission, contact the publisher at books@daveburgessconsulting.com.

> This book is available at special discounts when purchased in quantity for educational purposes or for use as premiums, promotions, or fundraisers. For inquiries and details, contact the publisher at books@daveburgessconsulting.com.

Published by Dave Burgess Consulting, Inc.
San Diego, CA
DaveBurgessConsulting.com

Library of Congress Control Number: 2023947782
Paperback ISBN: 978-1-956306-59-0
Ebook ISBN: 978-1-956306-60-6

Cover and interior design by Liz Schreiter
Edited and produced by Reading List Editorial
ReadingListEditorial.com

To my mom.
Maman, thank you for teaching me how to be a strong woman and a great mother. Your constant support through the highs and lows means the world. Je t'aime.

To my boys.
Caden, Emmett, Brooks, and Brecken, thank you for giving me the best job. Being your mom is the most precious gift, and I am grateful for all that you've taught me. I love you more than you'll ever know.

# Contents

INTRODUCTION . . . . . . . . . . . . . . . . . . . . . . . . . . . . . . . . . . . . 1
*How Do You Do It?*

LESSON #1 . . . . . . . . . . . . . . . . . . . . . . . . . . . . . . . . . . . . . . . 14
*Meaning Is More Important Than Balance*

LESSON #2 . . . . . . . . . . . . . . . . . . . . . . . . . . . . . . . . . . . . . . . 19
*Self-Care Isn't Selfish, It's Necessary*

LESSON #3 . . . . . . . . . . . . . . . . . . . . . . . . . . . . . . . . . . . . . . . 25
*The Goal Is Not Selflessness, and That's Not Selfish*

LESSON #4 . . . . . . . . . . . . . . . . . . . . . . . . . . . . . . . . . . . . . . . 29
*The Value of Rest*

LESSON #5 . . . . . . . . . . . . . . . . . . . . . . . . . . . . . . . . . . . . . . . 35
*The Difference Between Rest and Restoration*

LESSON #6 . . . . . . . . . . . . . . . . . . . . . . . . . . . . . . . . . . . . . . . 41
*Accepting Help Is a Sign of Strength*

LESSON #7 . . . . . . . . . . . . . . . . . . . . . . . . . . . . . . . . . . . . . . . 45
*It Takes a Village*

LESSON #8 . . . . . . . . . . . . . . . . . . . . . . . . . . . . . . . . . . . . . . . 49
*Yours Words Matter*

LESSON # 9 . . . . . . . . . . . . . . . . . . . . . . . . . . . . . . . . . . . . . . . 57
*Sharing Our Truth Helps Everyone*

LESSON # 10 . . . . . . . . . . . . . . . . . . . . . . . . . . . . . . . . . . . . . . 63
*You Are Not Invincible, Just Get Back Up*

LESSON #11 . . . . . . . . . . . . . . . . . . . . . . . . . . . . . . . . . . . . . . 68
*You Are Worth the Work*

LESSON #12 .................................................. 75
*Self-Care Is Not Enough: Find Your Stressors and Lessen or Fix Them*

LESSON #13 .................................................. 83
*Set and Respect Limits and Boundaries*

LESSON #14 .................................................. 88
*Follow Your Passions*

LESSON #15 .................................................. 95
*Habits, Small Goals, and Big Results*

LESSON #16 .................................................. 102
*You Are Great, Own It*

LESSON #17 .................................................. 106
*Stop the Comparison—It's a Trap*

LESSON #18 .................................................. 110
*Remember the Good*

LESSON #19 .................................................. 116
*Small Actions, Big Impact*

LESSON #20 .................................................. 121
*You ARE Making a Difference*

LESSON #21 .................................................. 125
*Guilt: Feel It to Heal It*

CONCLUSION ................................................ 129
*I'll Leave You with This*

Bibliography ................................................. 131
Acknowledgments ........................................... 134
About the Author ............................................ 137
More from Dave Burgess Consulting, Inc. ................. 139

# Introduction

## How Do You Do It?

> *Being human is not hard because you're doing it wrong, it's hard because you're doing it right.*
> —GLENNON DOYLE, *UNTAMED*

**THINK OF SOMEONE YOU LOOK UP TO, SOMEONE YOU ADMIRE, SOMEONE WHO INSPIRES YOU.** Do you ever ask yourself how in the world they're accomplishing so much? How are they so incredible? Do they have a magical gift or have some kind of special talent? You want to be more like them and embody some of their amazing skills and strengths, know-how, and ways. What's their secret? What is the trick?!

Here's the truth . . .

There is none!

As someone who constantly looks up to others to get inspired and be encouraged, supported, and pushed, I am often guilty of drooling over other people's "togetherness." They make everything look so easy. Interestingly, over the years, some people have shared with me that they see me as one of those people who has it all together, who moves mountains and makes it look effortless. With that, I've also come to know that this is not reality, but rather perception. What you see, the successes, the final product, all the things that get done, those are just on the surface. What we fail to see is everything that goes on under the surface. Everything that happens behind the scenes. The blood, sweat, and tears. The hard work. The time. The stress. The sacrifices. The late nights and early mornings. People don't see those as often, which leads to a skewed perception or the illusion that success comes easily, quickly, and effortlessly.

I've also been reflecting on how I seem to be giving the impression that I "do it all." As a full-time teacher and mother of four energetic boys, the number one question I get is "How do you do it?!" People believe that I have some sort of superpower in order to do all that I do. The simple answer is that I just do what I have to do, which isn't a lie. I work hard, there's no doubt about it, but I work hard because I have to. My kids and my students are my world, and they deserve the world! But there is so much more to it than that, obviously. If it were that simple, people would've figured it out long ago.

Being a mom is hard. Being a teacher is hard. Being both is beyond challenging. Yet, you deserve to pursue your wildest dreams.

There's also an added layer here that doesn't seem to affect men nearly as much as it does women. This is why I've specifically written this book for women; I understand things most men and dads just can't. When my friend Melanie's husband goes on a business trip, he gets up and leaves. But when Melanie has to go out of town solo for a few days? *Okay, here's a schedule of everything that's to come during my absence. My parents will be here to help on Monday and Tuesday. Don't forget that Samantha has to bring her library books back on Tuesday. I've left them on the counter.*

And the list goes on. Melanie and her husband's realities are very different, aren't they? Her husband continues to move up in his career even though they have three children. He continues to feed his passions and interests by playing beer-league hockey and by going golfing without even checking what activities are on the calendar for the kids. Melanie holds down the fort, and although she is getting much better at making time for herself by working out and pursuing other interests, it's just not the same.

I love how my friend Erin talks about the emotional labor that moms take on. When their family goes on vacation, her husband packs his stuff, and, anticipating everyone's needs, she packs for everyone else. She also has the house cleaned and arranges for pet care and for someone to take out the trash bins and pick up Amazon packages. She alerts the school and daycare of the kids' absences—and the list goes on. She shares how the emotional labor adds up with everyday little things, like weekly meal planning or buying birthday gifts. When her husband helps by folding laundry, he has no clue which clothes belong to which son. He's never gone through their closets and added in new size ranges or decided when clothes get handed down to the youngest. Moms keep a lot of things in their brains at all times. It's constant, and we can't escape it.

Although I realize that this reality isn't necessarily the case for all families, I believe it is quite common for inequities to be present when it comes to gender-based domestic labor. There is a whole generation of women who have been brought up with traditional gender roles while also being empowered to be independent. These women take on the majority of house duties while simultaneously working. Men aren't held to the same standards. Dads are often praised for things like leaving work for a sick kid, waking up with the baby, grocery shopping, packing lunches, watching kids solo, and taking the kids to the doctor's. These exact same things are considered the bare minimum for mothers. One day, Melanie told me something that was hilarious and stuck because it proves this point perfectly: "In my next life, I am coming back as a husband."

Although it's certainly not always the case, I believe there are definitely more examples of men who continue to pursue passions and goals once they've entered parenthood than there are of women. Is this self-inflicted; is it simply biologically more difficult for women to put themselves first? Is it a societal ideal that has transcended through generations? I don't know, but it's there. Regardless, you, as a woman and a mother, can pursue your wildest dreams. And you should.

Over the years, and through highs and lows, I have learned many lessons. I believe that it is these lessons that enable me to do all that I do on a consistent basis, without burning out or wanting to hide under the covers of my bed until the end of time. (Although trust me, I've been there—I just haven't stayed there!) My hope is that you'll find value in flipping through these pages filled with lessons I've learned. I intentionally organized the book so that it's easy to read, even for busy moms. Each lesson is its own chapter and has tips and tricks on how to apply it so that it can be useful right away. I've also included questions that are meant to help you reflect and implement change.

Contrary to what you may believe as a mom and educator, you *can* absolutely strive to the greatest heights. How? Be gentle with yourself, and let's dive in.

## The Day My Life Changed Forever

I still remember it like it was yesterday. It was February 14, 2014, Valentine's Day, and the ultrasound technician was walking back into my room with my husband, Chris, after getting him from the waiting room. As Chris sat down next to me, the technician closed the door, turned her monitor around so that we could see it, and uttered words I'll never forget: "I'd like to show you pictures of your babies."

Babies. Not baby. What do you mean *babies* plural?

Chris and I already had two boys: Caden was three years old, and Emmett was thirteen months. I was freaking out.

I was sent for this early ultrasound by my midwife for several reasons: I was showing way more than expected, I had miscarried twins between Caden and Emmett, and, truth be told, because my midwife had pity on me. She knew how scary it would be for me if I were to find out that I was carrying twins and that my family would grow from two to four children, just like that. She knew that I'd need as much time as possible to process and wrap my head around how it would change the life I'd imagined for myself ever since I can remember. For all those reasons combined, she scheduled an early ultrasound for me. I am so glad she did.

As Chris and I walked through the hospital halls and back to our car, I began to cry. There were just so many emotions, and I didn't know how I was going to be able to do this—any of this. I called my midwife and got her voicemail, and whenever we talk, even to this day, she shares how she vividly remembers listening to that mess of a message, where the tears were flowing, and the uncontrollable sobs made it impossible for me to speak in full sentences. Even as I write these words today, tears fill my eyes, because it was such an overwhelming moment in my life. I'm not going to lie; although there were some happy thoughts, it was mostly negative. The plan had never been four kids.

Before Chris and I got married, among many other serious conversations, we discussed the number of kids we wanted. Chris wanted two; I wanted three. So, our deal from the beginning had always been that if we had two kids who were the same sex, we'd try for a third. And so, when we had two boys, we followed our plan. Just one more.

But then we found out we were getting a bonus baby. Two for the price of one. Except that's not true at all. Two for the price of two. I needed time to grieve the life I had imagined for myself. I needed time to process how, in a few short months, I was going to have four kids who were four years and under. I needed time to wrap my head around how, for my one year of maternity leave, I'd be changing three kids' diapers, while trying to bring my oldest to preschool two afternoons a week. My mind raced.

*What about the crib? Not only do I need a second one, but possibly a third one, because Emmett won't even be two years old when the twins are due.*

*What about car seats and fitting everyone in one vehicle?*

*What about breastfeeding two newborns? Nursing one baby is demanding. Is two even possible?*

*What about sleep? Will I ever sleep again?*

*What about my midwife? Carrying twins means I'm now a high-risk pregnancy and will need a doctor, and I won't be able to stay in the care of my incredible midwife.*

*What about family vacations and staying in a hotel with a family of six?*

*What about my students? I literally just came back to work one month ago from my last maternity leave. Will I even be able to finish this school year now?*

*What about working full-time? Is that even doable with four kids?*

I could literally fill the pages of this book with all of my worries, big and small, and how I needed to reimagine how the rest of my life was going to play out.

But with time, I began to feel better about my new life and felt more and more blessed every day. There was still a lot of fear, but excitement also began to set in. Chris and I decided that we wanted to celebrate these two little peanuts and focus on the good. We decided to have a BaBiesQ, inviting close friends and family to share in our joy and excitement. The BBQ was planned for the Friday following my twenty-week ultrasound.

As this wasn't my first pregnancy, I had been for ultrasounds many times before. Since I was carrying twins and was considered high-risk, these ultrasounds were actually called fetal assessments, and they happened much more frequently than during a normal, healthy pregnancy. Really, though, the only difference was that the ultrasound was done by a nurse, instead of by a technician, and there were doctors on hand to look at the results right then and there, which meant I didn't have to wait for a radiologist to check them over and send the results back to the doctor's office. So, here we were. Twenty weeks along, and I was lying on the table with warm jelly on my belly, joking around with the nurse that she had two chances to not disappoint me. We got to quickly look over both babies before she started taking the measurements she needed, one baby at a time.

Twin A has a penis . . . another boy! Goodness me. *It's okay,* I thought, *there's still hope; one more baby! Surely, I'll at least get to have one daughter.* But, as luck would have it—and I fully blame my husband, by the way, because it *is* biologically his fault—Twin B was also a boy! Now, judge me all you want, but I had just been on a huge emotional roller coaster over the last few months, so this felt like another blow. In that moment, I had to accept the fact that I was going to be a mom of four boys, never getting to experience what raising a daughter would be like. But as the doctor walked in, that sadness quickly turned to guilt, which completely took over every fiber in my body.

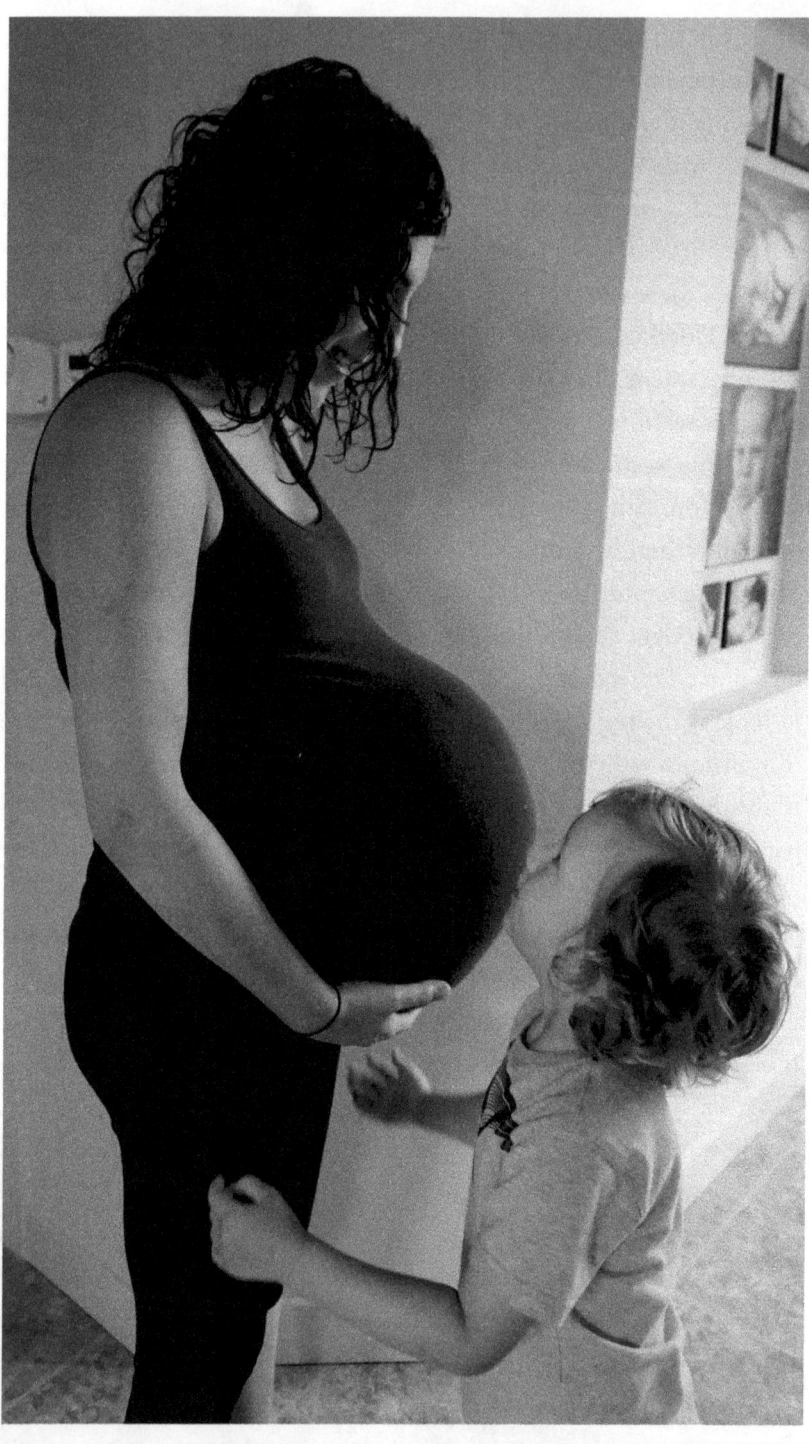

"Twin A has a condition called duodenal atresia," she said, "which we can see here from this bubble in the ultrasound image." We were told that this condition meant an obstruction in the duodenum, which results in increased amniotic fluid during pregnancy (polyhydramnios) and intestinal obstruction in newborn babies. This essentially meant that our baby couldn't digest food or have bowel movements. He would need surgery at birth to fix the blockage, enabling him to eat just like you and me.

Gulp. My tiny newborn baby going under the knife at birth? Panic. Fear. Heartbreak.

Put yourself in my shoes for a second. Moments before the doctor walked in, I was so concerned with the sexes of my babies that I had failed to focus on what is truly important. To this day, when people use the phrase "I just want a healthy baby," it makes me cringe. I felt like one horrible human being, and as though I was already failing at motherhood, especially as a mom of four!

In order to look further into Twin A's health, I was scheduled for an amniocentesis test, and I had to rest for the next twenty-four hours to avoid possible complications. I was back on my feet just in time for our BaBiesQ, which we were extra excited about, because celebrating these two peanuts was important, no matter the state of their health. Having that party was a breath of fresh air, getting to focus on the positive and celebrate with family and friends!

Fast-forward to thirty-seven weeks of pregnancy. I was a whale. (No seriously, I was and own it . . . twins *plus* extra fluid.) It actually hurts my eyes to look back on photos of the end of my pregnancy. Can you say beach ball?

I gave birth to two perfect little boys on August 29, 2014, who both weighed 5 lbs., 15 oz. Brooks (who had duodenal atresia) was born at 11:42 p.m. and paved the way for his brother Brecken, who was born feet first at 11:45 p.m. I was able to snuggle them both for a few hours before Brooks was taken to the NICU. Seeing as he had an intestinal obstruction, he couldn't breastfeed and had to be fed through

an IV. When he wasn't even forty-eight hours old, he headed into surgery so that they could fix him up, good as new! He needed recovery time after his surgery in order to heal and show his body what it was like to have breast milk run through his system. Brooks was lucky to have a twin brother who made sure to bring in my milk and ensure that my body made enough of it for two newborns. Little by little, he built up his feeds (and lowered the IV intake) and was able to come home with us when he was just over two weeks old—a true fighter, as we had been told to expect four to six weeks.

This whole story was obviously just the beginning of my new life's journey, and we've had many crazy adventures since. As I write these words today, my boys are twelve, ten, and eight times two! I went back to work as a full-time first-grade teacher when the twins turned one and have been working ever since. I can't say that that transition was an easy one, but little by little, we got used to our new routine and have been adjusting and trying to figure things out ever since. As the boys continue to grow, each milestone brings on new challenges. We are

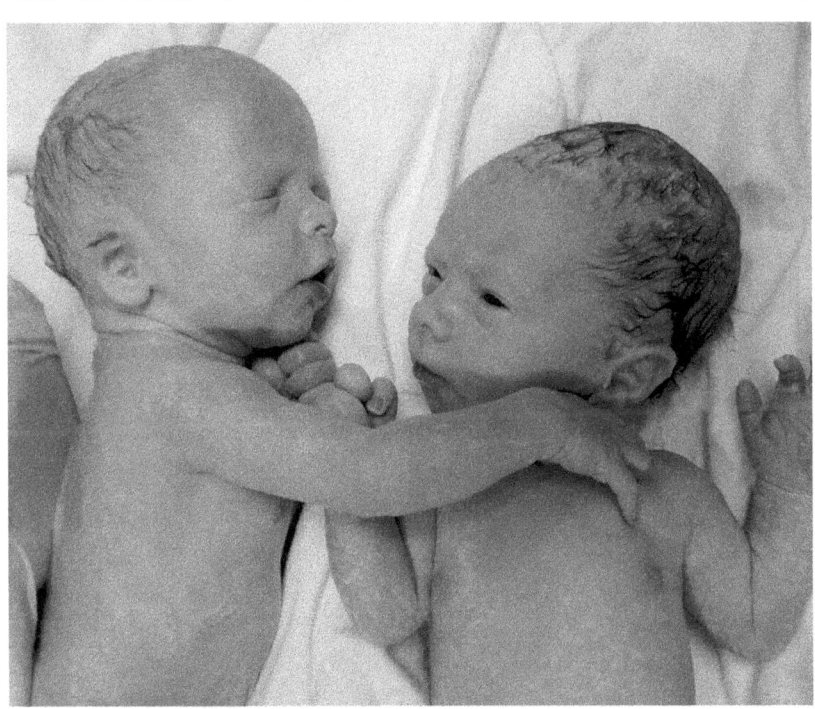
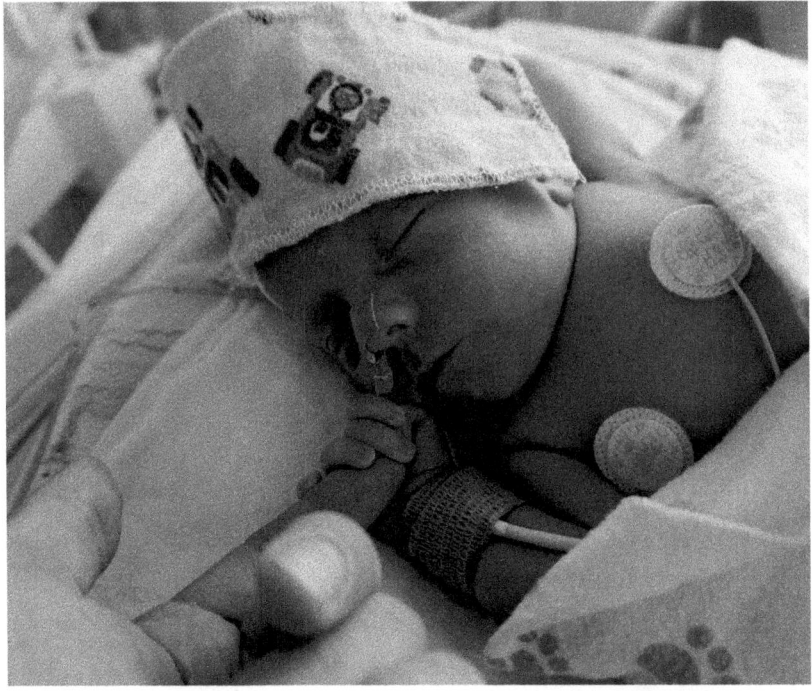

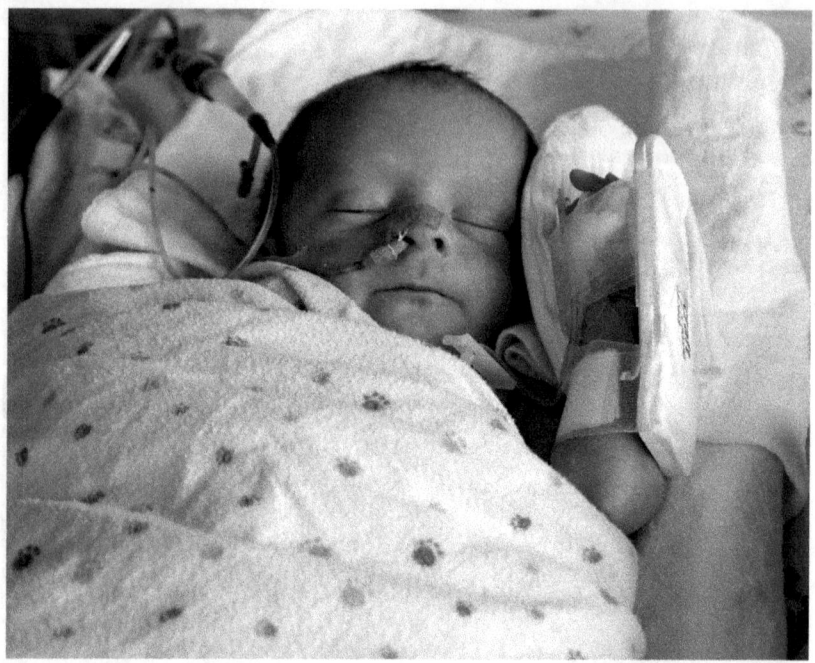

past the diaper-changing days but have entered the talking-back stage. The boys are also now all playing hockey, among other sports, so our evenings and weekends are spent running from one place to another, but we wouldn't have it any other way.

When people who only know me professionally find out that I have four boys at home, it's not uncommon for them to pick up their jaws off the floor. Not only do I work full-time as a teacher (which, let's be honest, is more than a full-time job), I'm an avid social media user, runner, blogger, and lifelong learner. From hockey, to swimming, to soccer and flag football, to homework, to family dinners and birthday parties, to parent-teacher conferences and exhibition evenings . . . Well, let's just say I am incredibly busy. I don't wear this as a badge of honor; it is quite simply my life, and I am choosing to embrace it.

I think the general perception is that a mom of four like me couldn't possibly do all that I am doing. But I am here to bust that myth. This book is not written so that you'll go and have more children while also excelling in this profession—unless you want to, then have at it! This book is written to show you that you, too, can follow your wildest passions and dreams while fulfilling your purpose no matter your circumstance. If I can do it, so can you.

# Lesson #1
## Meaning Is More Important Than Balance

> *When a woman finally learns that pleasing the world is impossible, she becomes free to learn to please herself.*
>
> —GLENNON DOYLE, *UNTAMED*

**BALANCE IS UNATTAINABLE.** There, I said it.

Balance as a mom is hard. Balance as an educator is hard. And putting the two together becomes impossible. But shouldn't we strive for it? I would argue that no, we shouldn't. If we know it's unattainable, and we continue to strive for it, we are always left feeling as though we're coming up short. Failing. Not good enough. Can't get it together. And trust me, as moms and teachers, we don't need any more reasons than we already make up in our own heads to make ourselves feel like we're not enough. I'm not suggesting that we throw our hands up in the air and just quit altogether, I'm simply wondering if we could reflect on what exactly we're after, and I don't think balance is it.

What if we embraced the fact that balance is an illusion and instead worked toward something more positive and productive: finding our center.

As Rachel Hollis explains in her book *Girl, Stop Apologizing*, "Centered means that you feel grounded and at peace with yourself. Centered means that you can't be knocked off balance regardless of how chaotic things become."

Letting go of striving for balance has been liberating for me. Finding my center has been much more productive. It's not something that I did once and now I'm set for life; it has and will continue to shift throughout my life, as it will for you. When I was focusing on growing my family, that was where most of my energy was. I used to find great pleasure in playing on the floor with my boys, soaking up all their firsts, testing out new baby food recipes, expanding my cloth diaper stash, learning new ways to babywear, and being the proudest mom, bragging about my littles' milestones every chance I got. My energy shifted more toward my profession when I went back to work after my last maternity leave. I was no longer looking forward to the next maternity leave and getting the time off to spend with my boys and my growing family. Instead I was looking forward to learning how to be a better teacher. I was then able to put more time and energy into what I did at school every day. I was able to grow there.

Don't get me wrong, it's not an either-or. The beautiful thing about focusing on being centered as opposed to finding balance is that if you are centered, you understand that there are moments in your life where you'll give more energy to one thing and less to others, and that's okay. When I was part of the team opening up a new school, I gave a ton of energy there and a lot less at home. My husband picked up a lot of the slack that year, holding down the fort and caring for our boys while I worked long hours. He thankfully works a job where he is generally home by early afternoon, which allowed him to compensate for my "shortcomings" that year. My parents were also fantastic in helping us get our boys to their activities and taking them for sleepovers when my husband needed a break. I would also productively utilize my time and work during my lunch hour and go back to work once my boys were in bed to try and maximize the time I could spend with them. There were sacrifices, but that didn't make me a bad wife or mother; it taught my boys what hard work and dedication look like.

The following year, although I still poured quite a bit of energy into my work, I was able to be more present at home, soaking up time with my growing boys while making up for the previous year. Sometimes your energy will be spent in a specific area for a period of days (report cards season) or even hours (your child's birthday party). Being centered in those situations means that I am continuously reminding myself that there's no reason for me to feel guilty for pouring more energy into one place instead of trying to juggle all of the plates I'm supposed to be holding up equally, according to others. Being centered means that you've looked internally and know in your heart that what you are doing works for you. Being centered means knowing that outside perspectives and perceptions don't matter because, in the end, only you know what is right for you.

Despite knowing that it shouldn't, placing too much focus on the world's expectations of you will undoubtedly lead to one thing . . .

GUILT.

It is something I feel every day. Guilt as a mom. Guilt as a wife. Guilt as a teacher. I think this is inevitable since I care so much and always want to do my best. Often, my struggle is that I *feel* as though I'm not giving enough as a teacher when I'm being a great mom and wife. And when I'm being a great teacher, I *feel* I'm falling short as a mom and wife. I think I feel this guilt because I'm not doing what everyone else is doing or I'm not doing what people expect someone like me would do. I often get comments along the lines of "I don't know how you do it," and well-intentioned people tell me that I need to slow down or cut things out because "You can't do it all/you'll burn out/you'll lose your mind/you'll (insert negative comment here)." These comments show me that people don't truly understand me, and although I know it comes from a good place, it is hurtful. People generally assume that working is taking away from my family life, and I can't blame them, because I often feel guilty about this exact thing even though I know it's not true.

What I've discovered over the years is that immersing myself in my work is sometimes exactly what I need to recharge so that I can be a better mom, wife, and teacher! As Adam Grant says, "Work-life balance sets the bar too low. No one grows up dreaming of a job that doesn't interfere with their life. We hope to spend our waking hours doing work that enriches our lives. A toxic job drains you. A decent job sustains you. A healthy job invigorates you."

What I wish people would understand is that sometimes, working is my "me time" and it refills my bucket, just like some people play sports or go to yoga to refuel. Of course, working isn't my only form of self-care, but it is definitely one of them. Maybe this is also true for you, but maybe it's not, and that's okay. The important thing is knowing what *does* recharge you and doing that regardless of whether others deem it to be the right thing to do or not. Self-care is extremely personal, so why would we allow others to dictate what we need to take care of ourselves?

So, although from the outside, it may look like I'm this wildly busy mom of four who works full-time and has to juggle her work and home life, working gives me meaning, and meaning is much more important than balance.

## #*PheMOMenal* reflections:

- ♥ Make a list of where your time and energy is currently going. Categorize those items based on where you feel your time and energy should go and what you are doing because of outside pressures. Adjust accordingly to do what is right for you.

- ♥ Your time and energy do not need to be distributed evenly everywhere.

- It's absolutely possible that what you deem to be self-care and what energizes and recharges you looks like it would deplete you to someone else. Be prepared for unsolicited advice, and practice responding by saying, "Thank you for your concern. I am doing what's right for me."

# Lesson #2

## Self-Care Isn't Selfish, It's Necessary

> *The state of your life is nothing more than a reflection of your state of mind.*
>
> —DR. WAYNE DYER

**SELF-CARE IS NOT SELFISH, AND IT IS NOT SELF-INDULGENT.** Self-care is what we do every day to take care of ourselves, mentally, physically, and emotionally, so that we are able to function and thrive. Self-care is not a distinctive recipe that everyone can follow; it is incredibly personal. What you might consider to be self-care might be a stressor for someone else, and vice versa. What recharges, restores, and rejuvenates you might not work for someone else. The key is to find out what does work for you and to do these things consistently, regardless of what others believe.

    I discovered the importance of doing this for myself in the middle of a particularly intense workout with my personal trainer. I was feeling strong, and I was amazed that I could do the exercises he had given me, including deadlifts, one-arm planks, hip thrusts with weights, chin-up holds and a slow lower, and finally, pulling and pushing a heavy sled. I was intimidated when he showed me each new exercise, but I was pleasantly surprised that the workouts I had been doing at home had gotten me to a point where I could successfully tackle this new workout! Then, as I completed the first new exercise in my next set, I hit a wall.

"Mike, I need a minute."

I must've looked like death in that moment because Mike told me to take my time, to take off my mask if I needed to (oh, the joys of pandemic workouts), and to go sit by the fan. I honestly felt so great until I didn't anymore, and it didn't come gradually—it was like a switch that just flipped instantly. It was bad.

Even after a few minutes of sitting directly in front of the fan, I didn't feel better, and I thought I was going to be sick. I made my way to the bathroom, and the simple act of walking there, dizzily, made things so much worse. I sat down and then really felt like I was going to puke, but I didn't even have enough energy to stand and pull up my pants, then turn around so I could be sick in the toilet. (Listen, if I'd been at home, I wouldn't have cared if my bare bottom was on the floor, but in a public washroom, where my trainer was checking in on me and could see under the stall, this was not an option.) I looked around and grabbed the thankfully empty little bag in the mini garbage can and had a plan to puke in there if it came to that. Eventually, the urge to puke passed, and I knew that if I could just get myself to sit on the cold floor, I'd start to feel better. I eventually had enough strength to stand up, but with sweat coating my entire body, it took even more energy to pull up my skintight leggings. I felt like Ross in that scene from *Friends*, the one with the leather pants and the baby powder. If you know, you know.

With some struggle, I finally got my pants up and was able to sit on the tiled floor. A few minutes later, I finally started to regain some strength. Although I'm thankful that I didn't throw up, I'm even more thankful that I didn't pass out—or worse. Needless to say, I didn't finish my workout that day, but what happened to me made me stronger in different ways.

As I reflected on that experience, I could think of several reasons why I hit that wall. But first, for context, it's not like I had just hopped into a super challenging workout without a base. At that point, I'd already been running for a few years and had been really focusing on strength training for three months before this workout. What surprised me the most was that I felt great until, all of a sudden, I didn't. It's not like I missed warning signs telling me to slow down; I just hit a wall like no other. But here's what I realized: my husband and I had been eating clean for several weeks before that workout—nothing processed, mostly whole foods. I wasn't super strict with my carbs because I had learned after week one that running with next to no carbs in my body made me feel awful. At one point during this clean-eating journey, I started wanting to allow myself a few treats here and there, so I decided to start using MyFitnessPal to track my calories. It was eye-opening. As I entered the food I'd consume in a typical day of clean eating, a warning popped up:

> Based on your total calories consumed for today, you are likely not eating enough. For safe weight loss, the National Institutes of Health recommends no less than 1000–1200 calories for women and 1200–1500 calories for men . . . Even during weight loss, it's important to meet your body's basic nutrient and energy needs. Oftentimes, not eating enough can lead to nutrient deficiencies, unpleasant side effects, and other serious health problems.

Oops! I never felt hungry. I was simply filling up on lots of veggies and protein throughout the day, but I was apparently starving my body and didn't even know it. That is the biggest reason why I believe I crashed and burned during that workout. My body was like, "Nope, you don't have any more energy to burn, lady, and if you're not going to stop, I'm going to make you stop."

Noted! I never want to feel like that ever again!

But then it got me thinking about how this relates to so much more than fitness and calories, but particularly to wellness and self-care. Food gives us energy, and without it, we are weak and can't be our best selves. The same is true with self-care . . . but I know that it is much easier to neglect self-care than it is to neglect food. The thing is, it's just as important, but do we prioritize it in the same way? Not even close. But we should, we really should.

We would never go several days without eating. Can you imagine? "Sure Joe, I'll do this thing you asked me to do during my lunch hour today, even though I haven't eaten since Sunday." You know where this is going. We are SO quick to put our own wellness to the side and never think twice about it. We need to stop feeling guilty about prioritizing ourselves and making sure that we make time for self-care.

For me, I have a long list of "Zen Practices," as Dan Tricarico, author of *The Zen Teacher*, would say. Sometimes it looks like snuggling with my boys and watching a movie, or vegging out on the couch and watching Netflix with my husband. Other times it's guided meditation, or a book, or music, while taking a bubble bath. Writing, doing hot yoga, or going for a run are also critical aspects of my self-care routine. Sometimes it means taking a walk while chatting with a friend on the phone. Other times, it's baking with my boys or watching them skate on the backyard rink. Sometimes, it's choosing not to engage on social media, or taking a break altogether from it. Working is also a form of self-care for me, which I explained in the previous chapter.

I'd say that the most regular and consistent self-care strategy for me is definitely getting eight hours of sleep every night, but other than sleep, what I need in terms of self-care varies every single day. Therapist Vienna Pharaon puts it this way: "Check in with yourself frequently and ask what is supporting your emotional and mental health. A reminder that what was supportive yesterday doesn't have to be supportive today. What is supportive for your friend might not be supportive for you. This is a deeply personal exploration that requires your attention." Dan Tricarico adds to this thought by explaining that "your Zen Practice could be gardening, fishing, cooking, or anything else that lets you focus on your passions, explore your obsessions, be in the moment, and experience flow."

I've also come to realize that I tend to manage my stress a lot better when I have a "light at the end of the tunnel." This could be as simple as looking forward to a little family vacation or a PD day that I'm super excited about. Sometimes it's planning to take a mental health day when I feel the need, or my favorite: when I can carve out enough time to go to the spa (which, by the way, is exactly what I did once I submitted my manuscript).

Not sure where to start? I truly appreciated the roundtable episode of *Teachers on Fire* with host Tim Cavey and panelists Dan Tricarico, Lindsey Titus, and Dori Katsionis. Dan shared about the 5 S's: stillness, silence, slowing down, space, and subtraction. These won't cost us a thing and can easily be infused in our day, even in the shortest amounts of time. Lindsey helped us understand that how we individually define self-care is truly important and that we need to be proactive versus reactive. I also appreciated her 4 A's: awareness of where we're at, acceptance of the feelings we have, acknowledgement of where we want to be/how we want to feel, and action to get there. Dori's addition of her 3 M's aligned perfectly: movement, mindset, and meditation.

So please, wherever you are right now, prioritize your wellness and self-care so that you don't end up hitting a wall like I did during my workout. Whatever works for you is perfect. Don't feel the need to compare what you do to what others are doing. Sometimes the simplest things have the biggest impact, and we shouldn't wait until we feel so desperate for self-care to do it. A little bit every day goes a long way. You are important. You are worthy. You are deserving. And we need the best version of you, which can't happen without enough wellness and self-care calories every single day.

## #PheMOMenal reflections:

- Make a list of what works for you as self-care.
- It might be helpful to separate the list based on things you can do daily, things that are quick, things that take longer, or things that are done less frequently but offer more bang for their buck.
- Refer to this list whenever you feel the need to give yourself a boost. Don't wait too long, though.
- Self-care is extremely personal. You do you, and don't worry about what others think.

# Lesson #3

## The Goal Is Not Selflessness, and That's Not Selfish

*It's not selfish to give to yourself as much as you give of yourself.*

—SUZE ORMAN

**YOU DON'T ALWAYS NEED TO BE SELFLESS.**

As Glennon Doyle says, women in particular were brought up to believe that being selfless is the holy grail and that it's what we should strive for, always. This is part of our taming. If we're not being selfless, we are being selfish. Period. And no one wants to be selfish, especially teachers and moms. So, we give and we give and we give.

As for me, I care a whole heck of a lot. I care what people think. I care what people do. I want the people around me to be happy, to be learning, to be cared for. I want them to feel loved and supported. I wear my heart on my sleeve, and I do all I can to make sure everyone is okay . . . even if it means that I am not. This isn't unusual. In fact, I would say this is typical for a teacher and a mother.

A few years ago, I had a very difficult year, which I describe in lesson #10, where big stressors piled on, so much so that the everyday, usual stress became too much to handle. Because I'm so selfless, I kept on plowing through, ignoring the warning signs. Eventually, my body began to break down, and I had no choice but to change what I was doing. That's when I started running. Nothing fancy at first. Small, manageable goals: run ten minutes a day, and don't miss two days in a row.

As the pandemic hit in 2020, despite my running, more stress began to pile on. With activities being canceled and remote learning starting up, as a mom of four boys, I had more time and more flexibility than I'd ever had. So, I began running more.

*I wonder what running a 5k would feel like?* (It felt like death, by the way.)

*I wonder if I could build up to 10k?* (I did, but not without rolling my ankle first, needing physical therapy to heal, and learning that pace is important, especially when adding distance.)

*Is a half marathon within my reach?* (Yep, even extreme wind couldn't stop me.)

*How about finishing a half marathon in under two hours?* (Nailed it. I feel strong!)

*What if I helped my sister raise funds for MS and offered to run 1 km for every $100 she raises?* (Done! Cue my longest run at that point: 25k.)

*It sure would be fun to join a group of Ultra runners doing a 100k to raise awareness for the homeless and see just how far my legs can take me, with minimal training!* (Bam, 30k done before most people got out of bed that morning.)

This was my progression over three years, and naturally, it's taken a lot of hard work and many hours spent running, lifting, and training. But do you know what else it's created? A lot of mom guilt: *I am not being selfless right now, I am being selfish.* I was able to control this guilt as it crept in, but that doesn't mean it didn't exist. It was always there, in the back of my mind, making me second-guess my running goals and the time, effort, energy, and hard work it took to make them become a reality.

Then, a moment of clarity: my family and I were camping, and as I was doing the dishes outside one evening, I heard my boys setting up their next game, while drawing a big line across the road with chalk: "Run all the way around the bay. It's not about speed, it's about stamina. You just have to finish without walking." Be still, my heart. My boys, my four boys, were playing a game about running, as they've seen me do countless times. They were cheering each other on and running together as my running friends always do for me. They were supporting each other every step of the way and celebrating as each one of them completed their laps. They didn't resent me for all the time I'd put into running; they were learning from my example. They were learning that taking care of yourself is not selfish and should always be a priority.

As Glennon Doyle says in her book *Untamed*, "My children do not need me to save them. My children need to watch me save myself."

I am working on it, and I hope you are, too.

You need to put yourself first. It's not selfish, it's essential. And just maybe, putting yourself first will take care of those around you far better than any act of selflessness ever could. Let that sink in.

Save yourself.

## #*PheMOMenal* reflections:

- Think about what example you are setting for your students and your children.

- Children are always watching and are learning from every action. What are you teaching them?

- Reflect on how you are putting yourself first. If you aren't, examine how you might do that.

- Taking care of yourself is not selfish, it's necessary.

- It's not an either-or. You can be neither selfless nor selfish. No one should ever expect you to give all of yourself to someone or something to your detriment.

- When your children are grown, do you hope that they will save themselves or rely on someone else to be saved? Act accordingly.

# Lesson #4

## The Value of Rest

*Hard work is important. So are play and nonproductivity. My worth is tied not to my productivity but to my existence. I am worthy of rest.*

—GLENNON DOYLE, *UNTAMED*

**MAKING TIME FOR CONSCIOUS REST IS A CHALLENGE IN A WORLD THAT PRIZES PRODUCTIVITY.** Yet, if we don't make the time, we could in fact be less productive or efficient than if we'd rested and worked. Harry Bell, a wise man I once worked with, shared a story one day that spoke directly to my soul. From that story, two words clung onto my heart: *well-doing* and *well-being*. Harry spoke about his exceptional talent of doing things well. He, along with what I would assume to be most educators, myself included, are fantastic at *well-doing*. We are doers. We do what we have to do, and we don't stop until things are done, and done well. We put our own needs aside to make sure that the needs of those we serve are met. If someone is in need, we are the first to volunteer to help in any way possible, even if that means neglecting ourselves and those we love. We often get the short end of the stick, while everyone else gets the best of us.

After reflecting on Harry's story, I wondered if we can truly be *well-doing* if we aren't *well-being*. Maybe, but I don't think it's sustainable. In order to continuously and consistently do things well, I believe we must be in a state of well-being. I'm not saying that we should start caring less and doing less, I'm just wondering if we would actually end up caring *more* and doing *more* if we put ourselves first in order to maintain a state of well-being? If we built in that rest, would we not have more to give?

I reflected on this after completing a half marathon for which I had not adequately trained. Exactly six weeks before the 2022 WPS Half Marathon in Winnipeg, my neighbor/coach/running friend convinced me to sign up for the race. Maybe *convinced* is a strong word. I was ready for a push to help me get my fitness and nutrition back on track, and this was it. So, moments after I signed up, I sat down and created a six-week training plan. Now listen, I don't recommend training for a half marathon in six weeks, but seeing as this wasn't my first go at it and I had a base to build off of, I knew it was doable. I just had to let go of any expectation of getting a personal record (PR) . . . gulp! Mondays were my rest days, I would do kettlebell workouts on Tuesdays, Thursdays, and Sundays, and I was keeping it simple with my runs and focusing on mileage and not speed work or tempo runs.

| M | T | W | TH | F | S | S |
|---|---|---|---|---|---|---|
| 21 March | 22 | 23 3-5k | 24 | 25 5-6k | 26 12k | 27 |
| 28 | 29 | 30 4-6k | 31 | 1 April 5-7k | 2 14k | 3 |
| 4 | 5 | 6 4-6k | 7 | 8 6-7k | 9 16k | 10 |
| 11 | 12 | 13 5-7k | 14 | 15 8-10k | 16 18k | 17 |
| 18 | 19 | 20 5-7k | 21 | 22 6-7k | 23 12-4k taper | 24 |
| 25 | 26 | 27 5-8k | 28 | 29 5-6k | 30 pasta | 1 May Race Day |

My plan all laid out, I went to work. I started on Tuesday, March 22 with a kettlebell workout, followed by a 4.35 km run the next day. I had to postpone the next kettlebell workout by a day because my legs were sooooore, so that workout happened on the Friday. Saturday, we left home early in the morning to drive halfway to Banff for a family getaway during spring break. I knew I needed to get a long run in, so once we made it to Swift Current, my family headed to the pool, and I to the treadmill. Let me start off by saying that I strongly dislike treadmills on the best of days, and that day was especially not my day. After 2 km, I paused the treadmill to have a sip of water and immediately got lightheaded and felt like I was going to pass out. Not wanting to embarrass myself in front of the two other people in the room, I grabbed my water and darted out to the hallway, only to realize that I'd left my room key in the treadmill. The door had already closed and locked. I was seeing stars. Not good. I took a breather and then asked a lady walking down the hall if I could use her key just to get back into the workout room. I quickly grabbed my own key out of the treadmill and finally made my way back to my hotel room. It took me a long time to get rid of the nausea I was feeling. I sat there and breathed and eventually started to feel better. No long run for me. Such a great start to my already very short half marathon training plan.

The next morning, we hit the road again and made our way to Drumheller. We had a really nice day there exploring and hiking, and we then drove to Calgary. With a full day, a run didn't happen and neither did a workout, but I was okay with that, because after the treadmill incident, I could tell my body needed rest.

Monday morning came, and I woke up with a sore throat. COVID. And it made its way through my family. Happy spring break to us!

Long story short, COVID wiped me out. Hard! It was bad and wouldn't let up. I definitely got the worst of it in my family, as moms usually do, and couldn't even work the week after spring break. Once I did muster up enough energy to get back in the classroom, that was all I could do. I was out of breath walking down the hall. I was exhausted and ready for bed at the bell. And so, my training plan got left to the side.

My first run post-COVID was on Saturday, April 16, which was just over two weeks from race day. I ended up doing a very slow 10k with a few walk breaks and decided to let go of the workouts before race day. I managed to get a few 5ks in before race day and a very slow 15k with a friend to test out a new race day plan.

| M | T | W | TH | F | S | S |
|---|---|---|---|---|---|---|
| 21 March | 22 | 23 3-5k | 24 | 25 5-k | 26 12k / 2k | 27 |
| 28 | 29 | 30 4-5k | 31 | 1 April 5-7k | 2 14k | 3 |
| 4 | 5 | 6 4-5k | 7 | 8 6-7k | 9 1k walk | 10 walk |
| 11 | 12 | 13 5-7k | 14 | 15 8-10k walk | 16 16k 10k | 17 |
| 18 | 19 5k | 20 5-7k | 21 5k | 22 6-7k | 23 12-1k 15k taper | 24 |
| 25 | 26 5k | 27 5-7k | 28 | 29 5-7k | 30 pasta | 1 May Race Day |

As you can tell, I hadn't trained nearly enough for a half marathon, so I decided the best strategy was to go into it with a fixed plan—run for ten minutes, then walk for one, and repeat. I figured that I would probably cross the finish line about 2.5 hours after starting, which would be my slowest half to date by about thirty minutes. I was okay with that and had accepted it. I went into the run ready to soak it all up and not stress about time in the least.

I stuck to my plan, and every time I heard a chime telling me to walk, I did. Surprisingly, though, doing 10s and 1s actually didn't slow down my time nearly as much as I thought it would! Knowing that I had built in rest periods within my run allowed me to push harder during the running portions. I felt great throughout and really enjoyed the whole experience despite my lack of training. I ended up finishing in 2:05:48—a HUGE difference from my expected 2:30!

Interesting, isn't it? Build in rest within your plan, and you just may be able to go faster than if you'd worked nonstop! And the most beautiful thing is that this applies to so much more than just running.

Building in rest, breaks, self-care, or whatever you want to call it is not only necessary, but if used correctly and consistently, it may end up helping you do even more than if you'd left it out completely.

The value of rest is underrated, but if we remember that it enables us to do more in less time, maybe we'll be able to lean into it more easily.

## #PheMOMenal reflections:

- Building rest into your day can be as simple as actually eating your lunch during the lunch break or closing your eyes and taking a few deep breaths before the bell rings.

- With built-in rest, you'll likely be able to do more in less time by being more productive during those minutes when you are working.

# Lesson #5

## The Difference Between Rest and Restoration

> *It's the neglect of timely repair that makes rebuilding necessary.*
>
> —RICHARD WHATELY

**IT'S NO SECRET THAT THE EDUCATION PROFESSION IS INCREDIBLY DEMANDING AND CHALLENGING, AS IS BEING A MOTHER.** When people ask me how I'm doing, my default answer is that I'm tired. As a matter of fact, after giving this exact answer to my therapist recently, I came to a surprising revelation. I may wake up tired, go to sleep tired, and feel like I'm going through life tired, but I am not spiraling downward out of control. I am in control, and I am okay. To me, I am the "good kind" of tired, where I am feeling satisfied with work well done and feel good despite being tired. I don't mind living in this state of "good tired" right now because I know this season won't last forever. But what happens when it's more than just being tired? What happens when your soul feels injured, hurt, wounded? I experienced this several years ago.

It was Christmastime of 2011, and my husband and I and our oldest (our only child at the time) were between houses. We had sold our house, and when construction on the new house we were building was delayed, we moved in with my brother-in-law and his girlfriend, staying in their one-bedroom condo for three weeks. It was a little tight, but we were so grateful and made it work. Our parents and siblings had just found very special gifts under the tree—vouchers to be redeemed for a new grandchild or niece or nephew in August 2012. Everyone was ecstatic and couldn't wait to welcome another baby into the family.

Then, on January 2, everything changed. I began spotting and remember texting my best friend Nycol about it. I tried to talk to my husband, but it was hard, because we were sharing such a tight space with others, which made it difficult to have private conversations. We eventually made our way to the hospital and waited for what seemed like an eternity. Chris and I fully expected to be told that we were miscarrying, and it weighed us down. They did some blood work and eventually gave me an ultrasound. I was so early on in my pregnancy that a regular ultrasound didn't do the trick; they had to do a transvaginal ultrasound, which was scary. I was alone in the room with my thoughts as the tech did her thing. She warned me that this test could lead to a bit more bleeding. By the time we were done, it was late into the night, and my husband and I went back downstairs to wait for the results. The doctor finally came in and told us the most amazing news. We were not having a miscarriage! He went on to explain that I was just earlier on in my pregnancy than I thought, AND we were carrying twins. Sorrow turned to joy instantly, and all of the emotions we had been through in the last twenty-four hours seemed to fade away in an instant.

There was a problem, though. Over the next few days, the spotting didn't stop, and the bleeding got heavier and heavier. We knew this wasn't a good sign, and we found ourselves back at the emergency room over the weekend. During this visit, the doctor confirmed that I was having a miscarriage. We were heartbroken. The roller coaster of emotions was too much to handle, and although I was physically okay to continue on with my life, the doctor understood that mentally I needed time. She wrote me a note for a week off of work and explained to me what to expect over the next few days, since I opted not to get a D&C.

I was pregnant.

Then I thought I lost my baby.

But then I found out I hadn't and was actually blessed to be carrying twins.

And finally, I lost not one but two babies.

All in the span of a week.

It was a hard week.

I was tired and wounded.

Next thing I knew, I was sitting in my principal's office the following Monday morning, the first day back at school after the winter break. With tears in my eyes that quickly turned into sobs, I said, "Marc, this isn't how I had imagined this conversation would go. I should be sitting here today announcing that I am pregnant, but instead, I am sitting here telling you that I need time off work because I just lost my babies."

I remember then sitting in the library as tears rolled down my cheeks, because even when life is hard, teachers must plan for their subs. I felt so guilty that I hadn't seen my students in two weeks, and that I wasn't going to be there to welcome them back to school after the break. I felt selfish for needing time to grieve. My students needed me, for routine's sake. And I wasn't able to be there for them. I was abandoning them. I truly felt like the world was collapsing all around me.

I finished planning and went "home," where I spent the next four days lying in bed, alternating between crying and sleeping. I was able to speak to someone on the phone who had had a miscarriage, in order to process my feelings. It helped a little, but not much. And then I remember getting up to go to the bathroom, and as I walked there, I felt it. I felt my babies falling out of me. I couldn't help but cry as I stared at this little ball of tissue that was supposed to grow into two perfect little babies . . . and I just didn't have it in me to throw it out. So, I wrapped it up and packed it away and brought it with me to my doctor's appointment. "Can you please take care of this for me? I just can't throw it out, or flush it." My doctor was kind and replied that she would send it away for testing, even though we both knew that she was just going to discard it after I left. I was grateful for her kind, considerate, and compassionate heart.

I continued to go for blood tests until my hormone levels were back to normal. This was to make sure that everything did come out and that I didn't need a D&C. Every blood test reminded me that I should still be pregnant, but that I wasn't.

By the time Friday came around, I was ready for a distraction, and although I was still very much grieving, I knew that spending time with my students would do me some good. I emailed my principal, asking him to let the staff know what had happened and to ask them not to bring it up. I wasn't ready yet, but I needed some normalcy back in my life, and being back in the classroom, doing what I love, was it!

I put my brave face on and went to work. That was the best decision I could've ever made. My students were so happy to see me, and I was so happy to reconnect with them after a very difficult two weeks. I'm not going to lie, though, I teared up several times when I thought about everything, but I was in class, with my other kids, and that was a blessing. I had been so worried that I had failed them by not being there after the break but found them to be completely fine going on without me. Life didn't end for them when I just needed a bit of time, grace, self-care, and restoration. I didn't realize it then, but I do now: that little moment in time, although it seemed to be my *whole* life in the moment, was truly only a tiny little piece of their (and my) life.

As teachers, it's in our nature to beat ourselves up when we have to take care of ourselves. We are givers, we want what is best for our kids, and when we need time, it makes us feel guilty. Moments pass, and your students will be okay without you. Take care of you. I can guarantee you that if I hadn't taken those four days, I would've been no good to my students during that time. I took the time I needed and was better for it afterward. Our students deserve the best we have to offer, and in order to do that, we need to take care of ourselves.

# Lesson #5: The Difference Between Rest and Restoration

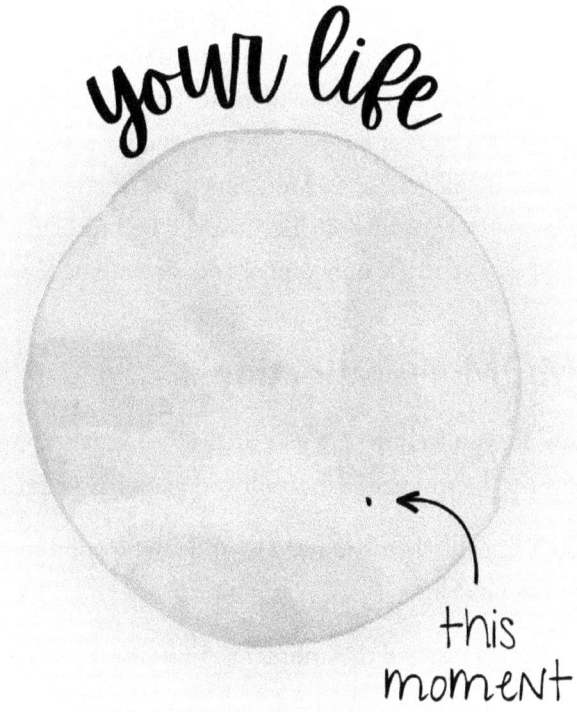

So yes, rest is important and can look very different for everyone. Like I shared in the previous chapter, built-in rest pays off more than you'd expect. Knowing the difference between needing rest and needing more than that is crucial. When you're mentally or emotionally injured, hurt, or wounded, rest alone won't get you back on your feet, or if it does, you might be more likely to get injured again, or it might take you longer to heal than if you'd done the work to properly heal. It might require you to look inward and remove toxic situations from your life or cut out other habits and behaviors that aren't serving you anymore. You might need to have hard and uncomfortable conversations to release some stress you're carrying. Or it might require being built back up by a community of people who see your worth and value, whether that be friends, family, or a therapist. Lean on them. No one is immune from being wounded or hurt. It happens to us all, so it's critical to know what restores us and who we can turn to in times of need. We are no good to anyone when we are down and out; we need to make sure we replenish our own cups so that we can continue to give to others, too. It will get better. Moments pass. And remember that this is just a tiny part of your whole life. You will be fine. They will be fine. Take care of you. There is only one of you, and we need you.

## #PheMOMenal reflections:

- How are you feeling? Are you tired or wounded? Do you need to rest or to be restored? How will you get what you need?

- Take time off when you need it. You are no good to others when you are unwell.

- Moments pass, and this moment is just a tiny part of your whole life.

- What are signs that you are tired and need rest?

- What are signs that you are wounded and need to be restored?

# Lesson #6

## Accepting Help Is a Sign of Strength

*Neither refuse to give help when it is needed, nor refuse to accept it when it is offered.*

–LLOYD ALEXANDER

**HELP IS A WORD WE SEE IN ACTION OFTEN IN A HOUSE WITH CHILDREN AND IN A CLASSROOM.** Offering help and witnessing classmates and siblings helping one another truly is a beautiful thing. (Maybe this is something we wished we saw more of between siblings at home, but hey, they have their sweet moments, okay?) Why is it then that as adults, we have a hard time accepting help and an even harder time seeking it out? I don't know about you, but when I am able to help someone, it makes me feel incredible. Maybe it would help if we reminded ourselves that giving help and accepting it creates a win-win situation for everyone involved. This became clear for me during a long weekend camping trip one rainy May.

Back in our early camping days, when we owned a tent camper and our twins were still in diapers, we went camping as a family. That May, we thankfully enjoyed a day and a half of good weather before it turned cold and rainy. When we woke up that Sunday morning, the forecast wasn't promising, so after breakfast and a few games, we decided to pack up. My husband went outside in the rain, and I packed the inside of the camper while trying to keep the kids happy despite their being confined to a small space.

When it was time to fold down the tent trailer, I got the kids settled in the van, and then the fun began outside in the pouring rain. (For me, anyways—my husband was already soaked.) After a few minutes, our campground neighbor from across the street came over. He was outfitted in his rain jacket and simply asked, "How can I help?" but it was really more of a statement. At first, I felt bad accepting his help; he could be nice and warm and dry in his own camper! I told him that we were packing up because riding out the bad weather seemed like the worst idea, with four small boys who couldn't be easily entertained inside the camper. He told me he remembered the days of packing up in the rain with a pop-up camper when his three girls were small—they were now all teenagers and could read, play games, etc. when rainy days came along during a camping trip—so he was more than happy to help. He then proceeded to help us pack up, right up until our camper was hooked up to the hitch and we were ready to drive off. What a kind, empathetic man!

Fast-forward five years: it was a Saturday morning, and I was rushing around cleaning and getting the house ready for my son's ninth birthday party with our family. I was also reminding my boys to get on with their chores because getting ready for a party is a family affair in this house—and we had a hockey game, a practice, and a team-building outing to get to before hosting the party. We had one hour left to get the house ready before the rat race for the day began, where we'd eventually get home just in time to greet our guests.

Through the chaos and as I was literally scrubbing toilets, my watch dinged, and a text came in from my dad: *As you are preparing for Emmett's party today, would you like me to take him to his practice?*

I thought about it as I continued cleaning and decided to take him up on his offer. Thank goodness for dirty hands not allowing me to respond immediately saying we were good, because that was absolutely my first thought. You see, there was no reason I couldn't take Emmett to his practice. My husband was taking the twins to their game, my oldest was being picked up by his coach for his team-building outing, and I was planning to go to Emmett's practice. Everything was all set, and I could . . . but it didn't mean I should.

I replied to my dad, thanking him, and he picked Emmett up not long thereafter and brought me a coffee. This gave me more time to tidy up around the house and get ready for the party—in a completely different state of mind. The stress was gone. The rush was gone. And I could actually enjoy getting everything ready. I even had enough mental space and energy to practice self-care by writing before everyone got home.

During the party, I thanked my dad again and said, "Thank you for everything you do for us, Dad. I appreciate you and love you very much."

His response taught me that when you let someone help you, you are allowing them to fill their cups, too: "Don't forget that I do this just as much for myself. I really love being with your family and seeing the boys grow up."

I am willing to bet that the man who helped us pack up in the rain felt a great deal of joy after helping us, fully knowing how incredible this gesture was for us, as he had probably wished for or experienced this kind of help many years prior with his own family.

In her book *Evolving with Gratitude*, Lainie Rowell talks about her struggles with indebtedness:

> When someone does something nice for me, I often feel guilt and an urgency to reciprocate (possibly even outdo their kindness). If someone pays me a compliment, I tend to deflect or downplay whatever the compliment was for. If I'm having lunch with someone and they offer to pick up the check, I might insist on getting it. (Even when my

original plan was for us to split it.) In doing this, I rob the other person of the joy of gratitude, and knowing this, I don't feel great either.

Is it possible that someone needs your help? Could it be that you've already been in their shoes and know how to help them get to where they want to go? Could something seemingly obvious to you have a huge impact on someone else if you were to share it with them? Maybe you can share which path worked for you. Maybe you are the push and support they need to get moving! Maybe someone just needs an ear, or a shoulder to lean on!

Or maybe you are the one who needs help. If you are reluctant to accept help, or don't feel comfortable seeking it out, I invite you to consider the other person's perspective and reframe it that way. Could you be taking joy away from someone by refusing their help? I also invite you to remember that, when you are in a position to help, you will, but until then, let others help you, because there's a good chance that they were once in your shoes, and you will be in theirs one day, too.

## #*PheMOMenal* reflections:

- ♥ The next time someone offers you kindness, accept it, and as Kim Bearden says in her book *Talk to Me*, "Say thank you, smile, and let it wash over you. Then pour your thanks over someone else."

- ♥ When you let others help you, it's a win-win: you feel supported, and they get to experience the joy of helping.

# Lesson #7

## It Takes a Village

*At times, our own light goes out and is rekindled by a spark from another person. Each of us has cause to think with deep gratitude of those who have lighted the flame within us.*

—ALBERT SCHWEITZER

**IT DIDN'T TAKE ME LONG TO LEARN THAT I CAN'T DO IT ALONE.** I need a village. We all need a village. Despite being surrounded by people, it's still possible to feel very isolated, and we need to be intentional about making different choices that will serve us better moving forward. Moms of new babies might be home for days at a time by themselves, the extent of their adult interactions being with the grocery store checkout clerk or their partner in the evenings. The same can sometimes be said for teachers, who despite being in a school full of people might feel isolated in their classrooms. We need to be intentional about building the chosen family we can rely on and lean on for support. In this day in age, and with the help of technology, finding people who align with our values and beliefs, whom we can relate to, and who can support us through thick and thin, is easier than ever.

When my oldest son was born thirteen years ago, I felt completely alone. Isolated. Even the postpartum nurse who was supposed to come over and check in on us changed every time for some reason. There was no consistency in the help and advice I got. In fact, it was often contradictory. I was a first-time mom and was not getting the support I needed. Although my own mom was invaluable during this time, she could only do so much and is not a nurse, so I ended up feeling like a failure most of the time . . . especially during my son's first three weeks of life.

When my second was born two and a half years later, I'd learned a lot and made different decisions in order to avoid the isolation I'd experienced the first time around. This made all the difference. I had a midwife instead of a doctor, and she had followed me closely during the pregnancy as well as after Emmett was born. She was available to me and was someone I could consistently turn to when I needed help with anything pregnancy, postpartum, or baby related. This is nothing short of extraordinary given the fact that my son was born on Christmas Eve. Had I been under the care of a doctor and postpartum nurses, who knows when I would've gotten a home visit during this holiday season, but my midwife? She talked me off the ledge on Christmas Day, visited on December 26, and provided endless support through the following six weeks.

Another big difference with my second was technology. With my second, I had a smartphone and was able to connect through a Facebook group with other moms who had babies in December of 2012. All of a sudden, nursing at 3:00 a.m. was more manageable because I could check in with them and ask some questions while answering others. Even though I was physically alone sitting in the dark nursery, feeding a newborn, I wasn't alone. I was never alone. I always had this great community of mamas who helped and supported me through the next year (and then some) right at my fingertips.

This very much applies to education and not just motherhood, and I think many realized this superpower during the pandemic. Sometimes, classroom teachers feel isolated, and when the world shut down due to COVID-19, we had no choice but to change how things were done. Teachers started coming together online to support one another, and collaboration grew exponentially. Educators who had felt isolated before got a taste of what it can be like when you have a professional learning network (PLN) by your side, whether it's in your building or miles and miles away, through social media. I know how powerful it has been for me to be a connected educator over the last several years, and I'm glad that more people have discovered this for themselves, too, even if it took a pandemic to make it happen. Teachers are givers, sharers, helpers, and finding your group of educators who will support you through thick and thin, through this pandemic and beyond, and help you take risks and try new things in order to do what is best for students is a *huge* positive from the devastating and challenging circumstances that COVID created.

Now, I've got my village, which is comprised of people who help professionally and personally. I've got family and friends who help get my four children to and from hockey practices, games, birthday parties, etc. when there is too much overlap and I cannot physically be in two or three places at once. I've got amazing colleagues who step up and do more when I can't. I have friends who bring their air fryer to the hotel we're staying at during an out-of-town tournament to help me feed my family on a budget. Another friend refuses to skip our yearly birthday endless shrimp dinner date even though I can't afford it right now and foots the whole bill. I have friends I met through social media who support me when I don't feel worthy, when I've lost my confidence, or when I need to brainstorm new ideas. I've got this incredible village I've built, that I lean on, and I have zero guilt around it, because I do what I can to help them right back. It is not a one-sided relationship; it's one built on the understanding that we are all just trying to do our best, and we will always help one another do that when we can.

This life that I've built wouldn't be what it is without my village. Find your chosen family. You, your children, and your students will be thankful you did.

We are in this together.

## #PheMOMenal reflections:

- ♥ Who is part of your chosen family right now? Do you feel like you could benefit from expanding it? If so, where is the gap and who would help to fill it?

- ♥ Some of my best friendships are with the parents of my sons' friends, because we are at the same stage of life and because we don't need to carve out time from our already busy lives to hang out—we're already at hockey practices and games together all the time! Could you foster those relationships to build your village?

- ♥ Are you a connected educator? If not, could you consider joining a platform and making some connections?

# Lesson #8
## Yours Words Matter

*Find a thought that serves you better.*
—DEENA KASTOR, *LET YOUR MIND RUN*

**YOUR WORDS MATTER.**

To others.

And to yourself.

But being mindful of this isn't necessarily an innate skill. It's learned from a very young age, and habits are hard to break.

Watching the documentary *Heal* on Netflix was completely eye-opening and also reaffirmed some of my beliefs. While I don't agree with everything shared in the film, some messages definitely hit home for me. This documentary explores how the mind is a powerful force that can and will heal the body under the right circumstances. It also made me pause and reflect on how powerful the mind is as a whole, which I believe we undervalue, especially when it comes to its correlation with our overall health.

Mental health has become an increasingly popular topic over the years, and for good reason. I've always been a firm believer that there's no health without mental health, but until I watched *Heal*, I don't think I truly understood at what depth our mental health can affect our physical health. In the documentary, a woman seemed to be doing everything right to take care of her mental and overall health, but after she got very sick and dug deeper, she realized that her mind wasn't in a healthy state after all. Once she peeled back the layers, she discovered things from her past that were still causing her a great deal of pain. I found this fascinating, and it resonated, as I've had moments similar to this, where I realized that things I had buried so deep that I didn't even know they existed still haunted me, affected me, and hurt me.

Although I had so many takeaways from this documentary, I was left with more questions than answers, and I longed for time—time to take care of myself, time to try different things to boost my mental health, time to peel back the layers to see what I could discover, time to heal, time to reflect, time to consider what I am teaching my boys and my students, time that, no matter the circumstances, I'd never have enough of. So, instead of getting overwhelmed with all of these new ideas, I decided to focus on one, just one: the impact of our words.

This is something that inevitably comes up every school year. Students (and my own kiddos at home) are not only unkind with their words to each other but also often to themselves. The negative self-talk starts to creep in, feelings get hurt, and I want to address it as soon as possible in a way that will be a bit less abstract for them. I've adopted an idea that I got from my best friend and colleague, Nycol Didcote, which I find to be super powerful.

- I start off by reading the book *Words and Your Heart* by Kate Jane Neal. (This book is available in French, too.) We discuss how our words can hurt and tear down, or uplift and make the world a better place.
- I invite the students to each cut out a heart from colored paper.

- We sit in a circle with our hearts in our hands, and I explain that we are going to say things we don't mean right now, just to learn what happens when we aren't kind with our words.
- We go around in a circle and say something mean to the person sitting next to us, at which point I ask them to crinkle up their heart. We continue until we've finished going around the circle and everyone's hearts are crinkled up in a ball.
- We then discuss what we'd typically do after we've been hurtful; we'd apologize.
- We go around the circle again, apologizing while students unwrinkle their hearts.
- Finally, we have a discussion about what we notice. Are our hearts exactly the same as they were before the hurtful words? Does saying sorry make everything completely better by erasing what took place? No. Our hearts have been impacted, and there is no going back to before, even with an apology.

- We continue on by discussing how we need to be mindful of our words and how we should choose to be kind and uplift others. This is just as important when we're talking to ourselves as when we're talking to others.
- The final step is for students to glue their hearts on a bigger heart, which includes the quote "Before you speak, think and be smart. It's hard to fix a wrinkled heart." I post this visual on our classroom door for a daily reminder of the lessons we learned through this activity.

> To save and print the Wrinkled Heart graphic, head over to annickrauch.ca.

This powerful activity helps me be more aware of my own negative self-talk, but it doesn't eliminate it. This is a whole other challenge for me, and I know I'm not alone. When a friend comes to you because they are feeling defeated, frustrated, and overwhelmed, or they need a listening ear and advice, how do you respond? I'd imagine you are kind, caring, and uplifting. You provide support while empowering them to rise above and tackle their challenges. Now imagine what happens when you are dealing with issues yourself. What do you tell yourself? Are you as kind, caring, and uplifting in your self-talk as you are when you're talking with a friend? I certainly am not, and it's something that I've been working on. After all, we speak to no one else more than we speak to ourselves, so this should definitely be a priority. When I catch myself in a downward spiral with my own thoughts and negative self-talk, I've started writing myself letters. This helps me to acknowledge my feelings while responding to them as if I was talking to a friend. It helps me take my own advice.

Here are two letters I wrote to myself in order to acknowledge and validate my feelings while also reassuring myself that I am enough. The first is as a teacher who is second-guessing her year's work as the school year winds down, and the second is as a mother who is exhausted from the summer break and is unsure how she'll face starting a new school year.

## Dear Teacher,

As the year begins to wind down, I know that all the doubts imaginable start to creep into your mind.

You are tired.

You are worn down.

And you begin to feel as though you didn't do enough. You didn't give enough. You didn't take them far enough. You weren't enough. And you begin to believe that you've failed them.

You question everything and analyze the time you've had with your students. You could've done more. You should've done more.

I see you. I feel you. And I want to remind you that you are enough. You did enough. And your students are lucky to have such a dedicated teacher who goes above and beyond over and over again. For them. All for them.

Worries creep into your mind because you care. You care so deeply about their success, however they define it. You are constantly growing and learning, so it is in your nature to doubt what you've done. This, although an incredibly valuable quality to have, also weighs you down if you let it.

I am here to remind you to check yourself and don't let yourself drown in your worries. Acknowledge them and let them wash away.

You. Are. Amazing.

Don't let anyone, especially yourself, make you believe anything less.

And you may not be able to see it now, but you have positively impacted so many students, who will go on to do amazing things—actually, they are already doing amazing things. All because of you. You.

Now, go rest. You need to take care of yourself so you can finish the year strong.

You got this!

Sincerely,

That same teacher

## Dear Mama (who is also a teacher),

As the summer break comes to an end, I know that stress, anxiety, and doubts start to creep into your mind.

You are still tired.

You are *still* worn down.

And, in the same breath, you begin to feel as though you didn't do enough, yet you did too much. You didn't give enough of yourself to your children. You didn't give enough of yourself to yourself. You failed as a mom, and you didn't even take care of yourself, either.

You question everything and analyze the time you've had with your kids, with your family, with your friends, with yourself. You could've done more and you could've done less. You should've done more and you should've done less. And now, the new school year is just around the corner, and you're wondering how in the world you'll be ready for this new feat, and if your children are ready, too.

*You can't even give your own kids all that they need when you're not working. How will you manage when you're back at school and giving all of yourself to twenty-something kids, too? Are your youngest two, who are starting kindergarten, going to transition well? Do they have the basics they need to start school? Will the one heading into second grade have regressed in reading and writing? Will the fourth grader, who is starting ELA this year, thrive, or will his confidence be squashed? Will your boys lose their curiosity and love of learning? I didn't prepare them. I could have done more. I should have done more.*

Mama, I see you. I feel you. And I want to remind you that you are enough. You did enough. And your kids are lucky to have such a loving mother who goes above and beyond over and over again. For them. All for them.

Worries creep into your mind because you care. You care so deeply about their well-being and how they make their place in this world. You are constantly growing and learning, so it is in your nature to doubt what you've done. This, although an incredibly valuable quality to have, also weighs you down if you let it.

I am here to remind you to check yourself; don't let yourself drown in your worries. Acknowledge them and let them wash away. And that guilt you are feeling? Let it go. It doesn't do you any good to hold on to it.

You. Are. Amazing.

Don't let anyone, not your kids, not your husband, and especially not yourself, make you believe anything less.

And you may not be able to see it now, but you continue to positively impact your children, who will go on to do amazing things—actually, they are already doing amazing things. All because of you. You. And they are so very lucky to have YOU as their mama.

Now, go pick your outfit for tomorrow and paint your toenails. This school year is going to be amazing, for you, your students, and for your kids!

And remember, you are positively impacting so many lives at school and at home. Not many people have the privilege of saying that.

Get after it!

Sincerely,
That same mama (who is also a teacher)

## #*PheMOMenal* reflections:

- ♥ When you notice yourself using negative self-talk, stop yourself and talk to yourself as if you were talking to a friend.

- ♥ Write yourself a letter as an outsider.

- ♥ You speak to no one more than you speak to yourself. Be kind.

- ♥ Mindset plays a big part in our life. Fill your head with good thoughts.

- ♥ Be your biggest cheerleader!

# Lesson #9

## Sharing Our Truth Helps Everyone

> *There is no greater agony than bearing an untold story inside you.*
>
> —MAYA ANGELOU

**IN THERAPY AND TRAUMA WORK, THERE'S A CONCEPT KNOWN AS THE "WINDOW OF TOLERANCE."** This phrase was coined by Dr. Dan Siegel, and it refers to the space where you can healthily process stress and intense emotions.

Do you ever feel like you're drowning and so you amp up your self-care routine to try and help you get out of whatever funk you're in? You try all of your go-to tricks, but despite your best efforts, things continue to feel hard, and you still can't catch your breath? You're likely outside of your window of tolerance. This happens to me, especially when there are either a lot of things going on in my life, or one major thing accompanied by many other small things. In fact, this happens to everyone, and people with fast-paced, stressful jobs (like teachers) can be particularly susceptible. That's why it is especially important that we reach out, share our struggles, and support one another.

In her book *Leading the Whole Teacher*, Allyson Apsey talks about the window of stress tolerance that she got from the book *Help for Billy* by Heather Forbes. Allyson took Heather's idea and applied it to educators:

> Everyone has a baseline of stress, and for some that baseline almost fills their window of stress tolerance. Baseline stressors for teachers include getting through all the content, making sure students develop mastery, managing student behavior, and squeezing every last minute out of the day to fit everything in. In addition, some teachers need to manage students who struggle with regulating behavior, disrupt the learning of the entire classroom, and may even act violently.

Allyson goes on to explain that we also have stressors in our personal lives, which we know as mothers are no joke and pile up quickly. It's no wonder that our window of stress tolerance can get very small and that we might reach our breaking point more easily. What's important is to keep in mind how we might increase the space in our window of tolerance, between our baseline stress and our breaking point, and practice it. This is going to help us tolerate added stress we experience throughout the day without creeping up to our breaking point.

It is also impossible to know every single person's baseline stress, nor do we know how big their window of tolerance is or what their breaking point might be. You cannot compare your reality to someone else's, period. This quote by Amanda Lynn Burkhart that I first saw on the Instagram account @TheMentalHealthAwarenessLife hits home.

> Maybe you think someone doesn't have a lot on their plate compared to you. But maybe their plate is smaller than yours, and doesn't have a lot of room to begin with. Or maybe their plate is paper, and their flimsy paper plate can't hold as much as your sturdy ceramic plate can. Or maybe their plate was broken, and is now held together with glue.

When I am feeling like I have very little space between my baseline stress and my breaking point, one of the ways I create more space in my window of stress tolerance is by opening up about my struggles. I don't hide away and pretend everything is okay, I share my hardships. Sometimes I do this privately with my therapist, or with friends and family, and other times, I share my words with the world through my blog. I don't do this to get pity or for people to feel sorry for me. I do this because no one can help me, and nothing will change, unless I am open and honest about what I am feeling and going through. When I am brave enough to share openly, perhaps at the very least, someone can find comfort in knowing that they are not alone.

It also helps to remind myself of Brené Brown's words: "In our culture, we associate vulnerability with emotions we want to avoid such as fear, shame, and uncertainty. Yet we too often lose sight of the fact that vulnerability is the birthplace of joy, belonging, creativity, authenticity, and love."

When the pandemic hit, the world got turned upside down, and teachers were no exception. I think it's safe to say that especially during this time, educators' window of stress tolerance was very, very small. There was a lot to process, and I was struggling. I noticed that many were trying to stay positive by sharing hopeful messages like "We will come out of this stronger." I was scared that we were saying things we didn't mean to help us cope and that these messages might hurt us in the long run. I feared that the world outside of education didn't understand what was being asked of us—of course they didn't understand. How could they? Had anyone shared, vulnerably and honestly, exactly what our situation looked like? I finally wrote, because I needed to. If I was feeling hopeless and as though I couldn't change the outcome of the somber future I was seeing for myself and for my students, at the very least, perhaps validating other educators' feelings, and mine too in the process, would help. Perhaps writing about our reality would help people outside of education empathize with us, show us grace, and offer us support. Perhaps sharing my reality would be enough to help me get through it.

And it was.

## Will We, Though?

Teachers are struggling.

I've noticed that we keep saying things like "We will come out of this stronger."

Maybe it's a way of staying positive. Maybe it's a way of reminding ourselves that nothing is forever, and that this, too, shall pass. Maybe it's a mantra that will come true if we repeat it often enough. Maybe it's a way of providing ourselves hope when everything seems so dark. Maybe it's the carrot we're searching for, or the light we are trying to see at the end of the tunnel.

The problem?

We don't know how long the tunnel is.

And I don't know how much longer we can keep *this* up.

*This* is a loaded word.

And if I am being completely honest, I am not sure we are going to make it. Some will certainly fall. Some *won't* come out of it, never mind stronger. The sheer weight that educators have been carrying since March isn't easing up. In fact, it is doing quite the opposite. Every day, every change, every new expectation, every press conference, every new announcement, every word that is taken back, every time we're told we're putting students first and doing what's best for them leaves us wondering, *What about us!?*

It all takes its toll.

We've been saying it over and over and over again. It was true back in March, and it's even truer today.

*This* is not sustainable.

And if we're not careful, it's going to crush us.

The Manitoba Teachers Society (MTS) polled their members and shared that "nine in ten Manitoba teachers were reporting high levels of stress this school year," and James Bedford, president of the MTS, said, "Teachers have reached a breaking point." In an earlier survey by the Canadian Teachers' Federation, Manitoba teachers reported that "stress, anxiety, and depression; workload; and mental and emotional exhaustion are their top three mental health concerns, as they manage the challenges of teaching amid COVID-19. Eighty-six per cent of Manitoba respondents reported being concerned about the ability to maintain their own health."

I worry.

I worry that as we continue to put on a brave face and "do what we have to do," we are sending the message that it's okay to expect these things of us. Teachers are givers, we have huge hearts, and we care so much about those we serve that we will go above and beyond to make sure that they are getting what they deserve . . . even if it breaks us.

Even if it breaks us.

And then what?

Teachers burning out and leaving the profession. Teachers trying to rebuild themselves in order to be able to serve others once again. Teachers dealing with new anxieties and traumas because their plates have been broken into a million and one pieces from being too full, for too long.

A reminder that comparison doesn't do anyone any good. Hard is hard. Period.

Students deserve our best. Is it humanly possible for us to be giving them our best when we are stretched so thin?

I am terrified.

The weight of the stress is unbearable some days.

"We will come out of this stronger!"

Will we, though?

## #*PheMOMenal* reflections:

- In what ways do you share your true, honest, and vulnerable thoughts?

- Do you have a journal or a blog? Do you prefer to chat with a friend or family member?

- I have therapy every six weeks, whether I feel I need it or not. That way, I know that no matter what, at the very least, I have that space and time carved out to talk things through. No shame in therapy!

# Lesson #10

## You Are Not Invincible, Just Get Back Up

*The truth is that falling hurts. The dare is to keep being brave and feel your way back up.*

—BRENÉ BROWN

**YOU WILL STUMBLE AND FALL.** Despite your best efforts, you will reach your breaking point. Everyone does. Contrary to what you may believe, this is normal. Even those people you look up to who seem to have it all together. And I think it's time we start sharing more of those moments to hold space for others who will do the same. The important part is getting back up, not the fact that you fell in the first place. By being vulnerable and both sharing and owning your story, you are supporting and inspiring other moms and educators to do the same, which makes us all better. Yes, being vulnerable is uncomfortable and scary, but educators and moms are the bravest people I know, so I know we can and will do this, for everyone's benefit.

As I've said before, I'm a firm believer that everything happens for a reason, and things happen at specific moments in time for a reason, too. Every once in a while, something happens in my life to remind me of this. It's not always easy, but reflecting in order to find out *the why* of certain events definitely leads to some powerful growth. Let me rewind . . .

At the tail end of April 2018, two of my boys got sick with the flu. So, I did what any mom would do—I took a family day and stayed home to care for my boys. By Tuesday, I was sick with something completely different, the nastiest cold I've ever had, and was too sick to work. By then, the flu had spread to another one of my sons, and we all sat and slept on the couch together, trying to regain our strength. This continued for the rest of the week, and although I was down myself with a cold that I simply couldn't shake, the flu continued to run through the rest of my family, but not me.

The following week, as things started to look up in our house, I went to work on Monday and headed out on a field trip with my students. Although my voice was still completely thrashed from my cold, I made do and we had an incredible day. I crashed hard that night because, as everyone knows, field trips take a lot out of teachers, even on the best of days. I woke up the next morning feeling off, but I shrugged it off thinking I was just worn down from the day before and still trying to get over that cold . . . only that wasn't the case. I had to leave school a little before lunch, but I thankfully had a sub that afternoon for a medical appointment. I went home and crawled into bed, thinking that I'd sleep for an hour before heading back out to my appointment. As soon as I hit my bed, though, I knew I wouldn't be getting back up. I rescheduled my appointment, and that was the beginning of a nasty flu that knocked me down again, this time for four days. Talk about a bad stretch!

In two weeks of school, I had missed six days of work, and it ate me up inside. My students and their parents were so patient, kind, and loving, and offered so much support. Although I felt guilty for being away from my students for so long, I knew they understood and simply wanted me back on my feet. I also reminded myself that when I missed school after my miscarriage, my students were just fine, and so my current students would also be just fine. I had to focus on taking care of myself. That Friday, I had just enough strength to get to work for a PD day, but something wasn't right. The previous day, while still at home sick, I noticed that part of my left leg was numb. I was advised by my doctor's office to get checked out at Urgent Care. I headed there after work, but a blood test didn't show anything, so they sent me on my way and told me to follow up with my doctor if the problem persisted. Saturday, I went on with a typical busy day, with two hockey games and a birthday party. By the time we got home in the evening, I was in tears and in denial. I knew something was wrong but didn't want to believe it or face it, actually. The numbness continued to spread and was now in the left side of my face. I eventually built up the courage to call Health Links, who wanted to transfer me directly to 911. I refused and told them I'd get myself to an emergency room. I called my mom, who came to pick me up, and we arrived at the hospital just before 10:00 p.m. A CAT scan showed nothing abnormal, which ruled out scary, urgent things such as stroke and cancer. Although that eased my mind a bit, I knew I wasn't out of the woods yet.

My sister was diagnosed with MS in 2008, and ever since my numbness symptoms arose, that thought had been in the back of my mind. I was sent on my way and was instructed to follow up with my family doctor because MS is a disease that is diagnosed by process of elimination and isn't "urgent." *Stroke and cancer are now out . . . what else could it be? It must be MS.* I was so, so worried. I got home around 3:00 a.m. and went straight to sleep. The next morning, my husband left with our oldest to get to hockey, and my dad thankfully came over to care for the other three so I could sleep. I managed to get through the weekend and chose to focus on the good in my life. I had a near perfect day with my boys celebrating Mother's Day, and although I had missed a lot of work in the previous two weeks, I decided to keep my personal day that I had planned months before for that following Monday. Instead of going to the spa like I had originally planned, I caught up on things around the house and treated myself to a pedicure. I was in no mood to sit with my own thoughts at the spa all day, so this was a nice alternative. Tuesday I was back in class, and I was SO happy to be with my students again. Oh, how we had missed one another! We had a great day catching up and figuring out where we were in our learning. Wednesday afternoon was my follow-up appointment with my doctor, and it was a hard day. The unknown is so scary, but I was also so nervous for my appointment because I wasn't sure I was ready to hear what she would have to say. She did a few neurological tests and decided that it would be best to send me for an MRI.

Several weeks went by, and the stress of being in the unknown was hard. As I was waiting for my MRI results, and just when I thought I was at my lowest, I found out that a mammogram I had at the end of May (my mom had breast cancer, so I get screened every year) showed something funky. I needed a biopsy and worried that I could potentially be diagnosed with MS and also have breast cancer!

At the end of the school year, my MRI results came in, and I was surprised and relieved to hear that I didn't have MS! As time went on, my numbness started getting better and eventually went away altogether. I had my biopsy at the beginning of the summer break, and I still vividly remember when my doctor called me with that news.

I was at a pool party with my extended family at my aunt and uncle's house. My cell phone rang, and when I saw it was my doctor calling, I went to find a private place up on their deck to take the call. With a huge lump in my throat, I answered, and she shared with me that my results had come back normal. I didn't have breast cancer. I hung up the phone and struggled to process these intense emotions while at a party.

In all of this, I felt guilty. Guilty that I'd not been putting my health first and that I somehow lucked out and avoided two scary diagnoses (more on guilt in lesson #21). But I was also incredibly thankful. I heard this wakeup call loud and clear, and it was now time for me to focus on managing my stress and anxiety better! With no other explanation, I truly believe that this all happened due to stress and anxiety. This happened during a very hard year packed with huge stressors—moving houses, changing schools, and opening up a new school, on top of the everyday busyness that having four kids brings on! In hindsight, my window of stress tolerance was miniscule, and well, stress and anxiety can do some unexplainable things!

When you are sick (or need a mental health day), take a day or two, or six . . . and don't sweat it. Students won't remember this when they think of their time with you as a whole. Be transparent—my students' families knew that things were rocky in my world. This is not a sign of weakness; on the contrary, it's a sign of strength! In all of this, my students' families offered nothing but support. You come first. YOU come first. And when you stumble and fall, get back up and remind yourself that taking care of yourself is your priority.

Falling down is part of life. There's no shame in admitting it or vulnerably sharing our struggles. Talking about it not only normalizes it, but it also empowers others to do the same. Then we can learn not only from our own experiences but others', too. Be brave. Be vulnerable. Own your story.

## #PheMOMenal reflections:

- You will undoubtedly fall; what comes next is most important.
- Get back up, but then be willing to make the changes necessary so that it doesn't happen again, or at the very least, so that you notice the warning signs earlier next time.
- There's no shame in falling. In fact, if you're able to share it, you just might help others in the process.

# Lesson #11
## You Are Worth the Work

*Every storm runs out of rain.*
—MAYA ANGELOU

**SPEAKING OF FALLING DOWN, IN THE NAME OF TRANSPARENCY AND SHARING THE GOOD, THE BAD, AND THE UGLY,** know that even the person writing about doing it all and thriving through it, the one who writes about self-care and meaning and guilt, the person who has many tips and tricks to avoid burnout, the person who received several clear warning signs about taking better care of herself, the person who's already fallen down and gotten back up, this person can still ignore all the warning signs, slip, fall once again, and crash and burn.

And I did.

# You Can't Stop the Rain

You can't stop the rain. Whether it's drizzling or pouring, you don't have control over it.

You can, however, grab an umbrella. You don't need to get soaked. You don't need to stand in the rain.

But what happens when it's been raining for days, weeks, months, or even years?

Is your umbrella still holding up? Maybe something that once kept you dry isn't anymore. Maybe it has a hole, a tear, or worse.

You can't stop the rain.

What if you are standing in the rain, and although you are holding an umbrella, all that's left of it is its skeleton. And you are getting soaked. The kind of soaked that leaves your skin so wrinkly it hurts.

Maybe you need a rain jacket, rain pants, and rubber boots. But you may be too soaked to realize it. You may believe that you just need to put your head down and accept that being soaked is your new reality.

Maybe you need someone to share their umbrella with you for a while. Maybe you need a gentle nudge to go inside and find shelter from the rain. Maybe you need time and resources to figure out how to repair your umbrella. Maybe you need space to realize that the umbrella alone isn't enough anymore.

Maybe you need a reminder that you can't stop the rain but that you deserve to be dry.

Whatever your rain is, know that you deserve to be dry.

You deserve to be dry.

During COVID, my family and I had several movie nights, as I imagine many did. One night, we picked *Encanto*, and I was probably more excited than my boys simply because the music in this film is by Lin-Manuel Miranda. Not far into the movie, the song "Surface Pressure" came on, and I was overcome with emotion. This song talks about appearing strong on the outside but feeling weak and being filled with anxiety on the inside. It also speaks of feelings of worthiness revolving solely on serving and caring for others. As a mom and a teacher, I could completely relate to this song, and, as tears filled my eyes, it felt like a punch to the gut. Let me explain by going back in time.

In 2015, I had just finished my last maternity leave where I was off for a year with my twins, who brought my total number of children to four. My light was shining brighter than ever at home, now that my family was complete. I was ready to focus my energy on my work—my passion as a teacher. I was heading back into the classroom with the goal of shining and proving that I deserved to be one of the few lucky teachers to claim a spot at a new, innovative school. I lit my flame, started my blog, and continued to plow forward. I found immense joy in my work, and that made it easy to do more, and more, and more, and more . . . I got the dream job and dug my heels in even deeper through that first year in particular, because opening up a new school places a whole new level of demands and expectations on educators. I didn't mind. The fire was raging in my professional life, and it filled me up! I was on top of the world, ready to climb to the next summit, and was even asked to do a presentation for my district on how my spark turned into a raging fire.

Gradually, over the years, I began to find much more success in my school work than in my home life. I was giving my all to school because that made me feel good, powerful, and successful, but as my fire continued to grow at work, the one at home started dwindling. I got to a point where being at home, with my own four boys, was so hard. I'd stay at school as late as possible. I'd be completely absent from my home life, even though I was physically present. My family was suffering because of it, but I didn't notice, because I was simply trying to survive in my own way, and the only way I knew how, by seeking out what made me feel good. That was work. That was being the best teacher I knew how to be. That was pouring into relationships with students, their families, and colleagues. And that was avoiding my home life as much as possible. I was numb to it. Eventually, the flame at home went out, and all I had left was my work flame. I felt like my only source of joy and light was work.

That was the voice of depression.

Then one day, everything went dark. I realized I had nothing left. Nothing. Not even a tiny flame or red ember.

What once made me feel good—my work—didn't anymore. As I was trying tirelessly to grow my dwindling fire, I was actually suffocating it. And it eventually went out, just like my home flame had. Darkness. I had no joy left. And worse, I felt like a failure. I couldn't even excel at what I was supposed to. I had been failing as a mother to thrive at school. Now I was failing at both.

Then, at a staff meeting, my principal shared that at their last admin meeting, their whole agenda got left to the side to talk about mental health because there was a huge problem in our division. This led to a mental health presentation, which I couldn't handle. I left minutes after they'd started because it was too much. I was crumbling and felt like it was too little, too late. The message? It's okay to not be okay.

*I AM NOT OKAY!*

But no one would know it.

Why? Aside from the fact that there is still so much stigma around mental health, it is also very hard to measure mental health problems and share these openly. Let me explain with an example.

A few years ago, my oldest son got a hoverboard for his birthday. I wanted to be cool, so I tried it. Well, this wasn't very prudent, and I fell. Long story short, it took over a week for me to get confirmation that my elbow was in fact fractured. I headed to the clinic to get my cast, but once the doctor there looked my X-rays, he told me it would be best if I didn't get a cast and instead started physical therapy right away to work on my range of motion.

This should have been thrilling news . . . but it wasn't.

Why? Well, it's ridiculous, really. I felt as though my injury wasn't as valid without a cast. Would people think I was overreacting? Would parents be annoyed that I missed some work for a broken arm that didn't even need a cast? Would people think that I lied and that my arm wasn't even broken? But my arm was broken . . . that should have been proof enough. And the pain I felt was real. Instead of thinking, *I'm pretty amazing for doing remote learning with a broken elbow, I am so tough*, I thought, *My arm is hardly broken, I'm such a baby!*

I'm weird like that, though. I also react this exact same way if I miss work and head to the doctor thinking I have strep throat only to find out it's "just" a cold. As if that's not reason enough to take a sick day. It makes me feel weak.

This whole situation got me thinking. This is my mindset when something is legitimately physically wrong with me. There is proof of my fractured bone. There are many X-rays that show the crack near my elbow joint. Every time I rotated my wrist or bent or extended my arm, there was pain, there was resistance. It doesn't get much more black-and-white than this. Yet, I still doubt. I still feel weak. And I still feel guilty.

It's no wonder anything related to mental health is astronomically harder. Nothing about it is black-and-white. And the doubt, weakness, and guilt that accompany it feel so much heavier. And so, it took me a very long time to come to grips with even contemplating a leave through my depression. Leaving behind what was the last source of joy I once had was scary. Feeling like I was selfish because I'd let my students and their families down shook me. The amount of work taking a leave would create for me was dreadful to think about. Thinking of the weight I would put on my colleagues if they were left to pick up my broken pieces was overwhelming. And of course, I questioned if what

I was feeling was valid or if I was just being dramatic and overreacting. Everything felt hard, and I didn't need more "hard." And then, my therapist said something that made me see things clearly: "Annick, we can continue to work on this bit by bit, like we have, if that is what you want. My question to you is, given your current circumstances—working full-time, mom of four active boys, pandemic—if you continue to work, will you have the time and energy to do the hard work that is needed to get you back on your feet?"

The answer was clear; something had to give. My doctor agreed.

The next day, I mustered up all my courage and went to see my principal. I closed the door and told him that I was not okay. I explained that I needed to step away from my job to fix what was broken. It was time I put myself first in order to rekindle the flame. I missed seeing the light of what each day had to offer. I wanted to feel the warmth of the brightness that seemed so far away. I was worth it.

The lesson here is quite simple, although perhaps harder to execute: know that there are better days ahead and that you are worth the work.

You are worth the work!

The work for me looked like going to therapy. It meant going on antidepressants. It meant eventually taking a leave from work to focus on myself, to rest, to heal, to fix what was broken, and to be restored. The leave created time that I lacked. I could now read, reflect, and do homework after my therapy sessions. It meant that my window of stress tolerance was bigger, and I wouldn't reach my breaking point before even getting out of bed in the morning. It meant I had energy to have deep and hard conversations with my therapist. It allowed space for me to examine my life and see what needed to go. It helped me find the root of certain problems and fix those, instead of putting Band-Aids over them. It gave me the space to heal. That is where I was, but it doesn't mean that everyone needs to or should take the same path I did.

You might not need a leave. You might not need meds. You might not need a therapist. (Although I honestly believe everyone should have a therapist. You go to the dentist regularly, don't you? You see a doctor when you're sick, right? I had a therapist long before my depression. Just saying.) You might need something completely different than I did, and that's okay.

The point is that you are worth the work, and you have to find a way that is right for you to do that work. I was able to find joy once again, which means that no matter how low my days get, I know that there are better days ahead. I can heal and grow, and so can you.

As I rewatched *Encanto* with my boys, the lyrics that first struck a chord in my soul now reverberate with a new refrain: Being of service to others does not define my worth. I don't have to be everything to everyone every day. There is value in taking a step back, catching my breath, and lighting my flame once again. I am worth the work, and so are you.

## #PheMOMenal reflections:

- ♥ If you are struggling, know that you don't need to stay there. There is light after darkness, and you deserve to be happy.

- ♥ You are worth the work. Determine what that work might look like for you. What supports might you need to put into place to help you get better? If it's helpful, seek the help of others (family, friends, professional) to find those answers so that you can get to work healing.

# Lesson #12

## Self-Care Is Not Enough: Find Your Stressors and Lessen or Fix Them

*The best way to treat stress is to eliminate the stressor.*

—UNKNOWN

**SELF-CARE IS A BUZZWORD WE CONSTANTLY HEAR THESE DAYS.** Although I am not disputing its importance, I think it's also crucial to consider what makes self-care so needed in the first place. We all live with stress at varying degrees, and even if it's impossible to remove all stress, there are instances where stress can absolutely be eliminated. If we compare stress to a wound and self-care to a Band-Aid, it's clear that if we simply looked at what was causing the wound (stress) and got rid of it (the stressor), we wouldn't need to use the Band-Aid (self-care).

As important as it is for me to share my struggles, I know it is equally as important to share the triumphs. If I can come out of it, so can you. There is hope.

As I prepared to head back to work at the beginning of February after my leave, countless thoughts flooded my mind: *Am I really ready? What if I slip back into the darkness? What if the stress is too much? What if I can't handle the pressure?* But I am so excited to see the kids again, to see where they're at in their learning. I've missed teaching. I've missed them. I hope they've missed me. What if they didn't? What if they preferred the teachers who replaced me? What if my family life becomes too heavy to handle when I go back to the classroom? What if I get back into the classroom and I don't find that spark again? What if I slip back into old patterns and routines. I learned a lot, but what if I can't put it all into practice?

Self-doubt. Excitement. So many emotions all wrapped up into one.

And really, there was no predicting what was going to happen until it did. So, with my head held up high, back to work I went!

I am so thrilled to report that things are going so much better in my life. Sure, there absolutely are hard moments and stressful times (I mean, I am a full-time teacher and mom of four boys, after all), but guess what? I can manage it! And it feels so good to be able to say that. I am loving being back in the classroom. I am happy again, excited about things we are learning, and my fire is raging. I also have energy for my boys after work and am not avoiding home life, but rather embracing it. Taking this leave to work on myself was one of the best decisions I've ever made in my life. I was worth the work.

One of the biggest things I've noticed since my return is that stressors that used to send me over the edge don't anymore, which means my window of stress tolerance has grown. A simple example: Anyone who knows me knows that I am super-duper organized and very particular, to a fault. (Yes, Dr. Keates, I am still working on not folding my boys' underwear.) As I went back to school to spend an afternoon in my class before officially heading back to work, I noticed that things in my room were not at all the way I'd left them. No one was to blame for this; mandates and regulations had changed, so students needed to be more distanced, and therefore the furniture had to be rearranged. Fine. But certain things bother me, like you can't have a tall shelf in front of a window, partly covering it. I can't handle that. But as I soaked up my afternoon with my students and the teacher, I let it go. I chose to smile and laugh instead of letting it get me down in the dumps. *It's okay. I can fix this when I am back.* But that was a huge moment for me, proving that I'd grown leaps and bounds. That one moment could have seriously set me back, and had I not done the work I had during my leave, it absolutely could have made me fall right back into a deep depression.

So, what changed? Well, first of all, I'd like to remind you that I did a lot of hard work with my therapist's and doctor's help, so if you're struggling, know that it's important to reach out and get help. I'd also like to say that I am completely over self-care being shoved down our throats. Wait what? Didn't I write a whole lot in this book about self-care?! Yes, self-care is important and necessary, but you know what's also important and necessary? Looking at WHAT is making us need this self-care so badly and seeing if we can lessen or even eliminate these stressors. Yes, I said it. And yes, I've talked a lot about self-care in this book. But it's not enough. Let's stop trying to put Band-Aids on wounds that will simply keep opening up. We need to reflect and try to get to the source so we can truly heal.

Naturally, there are things we can't control. COVID won't go away with a magic wand, and report card stress isn't going anywhere anytime soon, but I try to focus on the stressors I can control and what I've done about some of them. Simple tweaks can go a long way, and managing those stressors might leave us with a bit more space and energy for the ones we can't. Here are a few examples from my own life.

**STRESSOR:** Mom has too many responsibilities.
**SOLUTION:** I created a chore bucket for my four boys. We discussed that we are a family and Mom needs help. Our boys always did chores, but it was a constant battle of nagging and negotiating about what they were willing to do. This added a lot of stress I didn't need. So, the chore bucket was born. It's quite simple; we have two buckets, a "to do" bucket and a "done" bucket. We have large colored popsicle sticks, each of my boys has his own color, and the chores are indicated on the sticks. My boys know what chores they are responsible for each day, and it's easy to personalize it and change it as needed. They also

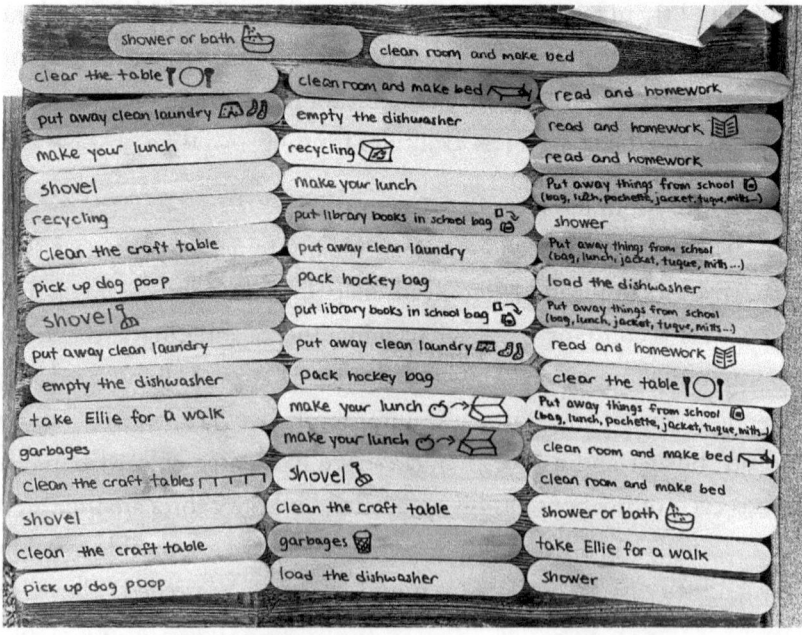

know that chores have to be done before screen time, which is a great incentive and reward that works for our family.

**STRESSOR:** Leaving the house on time in the morning before school
**SOLUTION:** Mom, after giving a few warnings (ten minutes to finish breakfast, five minutes, etc.), lets the boys know at 8:00 a.m. that they have five minutes to get ready and go outside. At 8:05, my timer starts, and anyone who isn't ready yet starts to lose screen-time minutes (because again, this is the reward that works for our family). If someone is ready at 8:06, they've lost one minute of their allotted screen time that evening. This has also provided a bit of a cushion so that if someone is having a particularly hard morning, we have built in time so that even if we are late leaving, we will not be late for school. If we have a great morning and end up leaving by 8:10, Mom has time to stop for a coffee! Yay! Having more time and not feeling rushed has been very helpful while trying to leave the house on time with four kiddos!

**STRESSOR:** Self-inflicted work pressure
**SOLUTION:** Less time on social media. I used to tweet about what was going on in my classroom often. Every morning before even getting out of bed, I'd also check out the school hashtag to see what was going on. I'd also read so many blogs and be very active on Twitter (now known as X)—liking, commenting, retweeting, sharing. While this used to inspire me and bring me joy, it somehow turned to pressure and stress over time. So, I've decided to take that out of my everyday routine. It doesn't mean I never do this, I just don't do it every day. The same is true for the pressure I'd put on myself to blog consistently. Letting that go has been freeing.

**STRESSOR:** I don't have enough hours in a day to do all that I need to do.
**SOLUTION:** Maximize my time. I used to do laundry throughout the week, but the baskets of clean laundry would pile up until the weekend, when I'd have time to fold (which was at least a two-hour ordeal).

Now, I've made it a habit to put the clean baskets of laundry right by my spot on the couch. When the boys are in bed and I sit down to unwind and relax with a show, my basket is there, ready to be folded. It's so much easier to fold one load every night! I've also been more intentional with how I use my time. My sons' hockey practices are a great time to get a run in, catch up on work email, or do other work tasks that I can do from my laptop. Mindless tasks that I used to do at school after work are now brought home for me to do in front of the TV at night or brought with me during lunch so I can do them while chatting with colleagues. It takes a bit of reframing how I think, but it has been so helpful! And I think it's important to note that not ALL hockey practices and evenings are spent doing work tasks. Sometimes I focus on socializing with parents or eating some popcorn while watching TV, because that's just as important!

**STRESSOR:** Mindless morning and night routines

**SOLUTION:** Being intentional about being present and letting everything go for a few minutes twice a day. When my alarm goes off in the morning, I allow myself to have fifteen minutes of phone time. After that, it's my dog Ellie's favorite part of the day—snuggle time. She knows that when I put my phone down and roll over, it's time for her to get really close and get tons of scratches, sweet talk, and dog owner ridiculousness! She loves it. I love it. And it helps set the tone for the day. The same is true for my nighttime routine. I've been having trouble with dry eyes, so my optometrist suggested I do warm compresses for fifteen minutes every night. Well, that's been a blessing in disguise! Fifteen glorious minutes to meditate, be in the moment, process thoughts and ideas . . . I've really come to love these fifteen minutes of absolutely nothing to do but lie there with zero distractions.

**STRESSOR:** Resentment that I feel like I'm always responsible for keeping our family organized

**SOLUTION:** Hold up, this one probably hits deep. Raise your hand if you're a mom who takes care of the calendar, places orders on time for school fun lunches, gets the kids to all their activities, ensures dinner is on the table at the right time between said activities, buys gifts for the upcoming birthday parties your children are attending, books parent-teacher meetings, puts clean underwear in your children's drawers, packs the special art supplies for a school project in your child's bag, purchases Christmas gifts and then wraps them and puts them under the tree in time for Santa's arrival . . . and the list goes on and on. I think you get the point. It's no wonder moms constantly feel like their heads are going to explode—that's a lot to manage and keep track of. My husband and I have learned that sharing responsibilities within our family so that not everything falls on me benefits everyone. He takes care of certain things, like adding the sports activities to our shared calendar, making dinner, and doing the grocery shopping, and I almost don't even dare say this, but he even does the Christmas gift shopping. (I know, I know, the meme goes something like "All dads on Christmas morning, watching their kids unwrap their presents, with zero knowledge of what's inside." Not our reality, but I know we're in the minority.) Having specific responsibilities eliminates resentment because what I need to do and what he needs to do is clear. Don't get me wrong: we help each other out in times of need, but unless he's asking me if I can make dinner, I don't even think about dinner. That's on him, and that's one less thing I need to think about.

Those are just a few examples of minor tweaks that I've made to lessen everyday stress that would otherwise add up. I'd like to invite you to reflect on stressors in your life and think about how you might make these easier on yourself. Let's rip the Band-Aids off and do the work needed to truly heal instead of covering it up and holding our breath until the wound splits open again. Self-care is not enough.

## #*PheMOMenal* reflections:

- What stressors in your life can you lessen or eliminate? Where do you have control?

- Are there simple tweaks you can make or new routines you can implement to lessen your stress load?

- Can you personalize or find inspiration in the examples I shared in this chapter to fix stressors in your life?

# Lesson #13

## Set and Respect Limits and Boundaries

*When you say yes to others, make sure you are not saying no to yourself.*

—PAULO COELHO

**A BIG PART OF STAYING CENTERED IS NOTICING WHERE OUR ENERGY IS GOING.** Energy is probably the most important currency we have, yet we don't think of it that way. Money? Easy. We're very mindful of what we spend our money on. Will it be worth our return? Will it provide us joy? Stress? Do we need it? Want it? Are we investing to guarantee stability later? We don't ever really throw money away. But what if we were as mindful with our energy? What if we really took a look at where we spend our energy and if the return we're getting is worth the expenditure? Balance leads us to believe that we need to distribute our energy evenly and equally. Being centered allows more flexibility as to where the energy is being spent throughout our lives. However, it is still incredibly important to be thoughtful and intentional about where our energy is going.

As Emily Maroutian explains in *Thirty*, "Energy is the currency of the universe. When you 'pay' attention to something, you buy that experience. So when you allow your consciousness to focus on someone or something that annoys you, you feed it your energy, and it reciprocates with the experience of being annoyed. Be selective in your focus because your attention feeds the energy of it and keeps it alive, not just within you, but in the collective consciousness as well."

Though I didn't know it at the time, I began to learn this valuable lesson when I was only in sixth grade. My mom had two severe depressions that year. I remember her going to live with my grandparents for a while, close family and friends bringing us meals, and going for family counseling. Other than that, though, I don't remember much else. What I've come to realize as an adult is that going through this as a child affected me more than I knew. I had intentionally blocked out many memories from that time, and it is only in the last few years that they have surfaced. Through therapy and talking to my mom, I was able to work through this pain, begin to put the pieces back together, and heal. Although that time when I was younger was very hard on my family and me, I truly believe that it all made us so much stronger. My mom is the strongest person I know, and through her depression, through her struggles, she learned a great deal about herself, which my siblings and I inherently learned as well. I admire my mom beyond words for always putting herself first now. She knows herself so well and respects her limits and boundaries better than anyone else I know. She is a constant reminder of self-respect and not caring what other people think. My mom is my rock. She, by the way, is also a mother of four. If she can do it, I can do it.

As I continue to learn and grow, and as the years pass by, what my mom instilled in me is always in the back of my head. I'm more mindful of where my energy goes and who I spend my time on and with.

As educator Angela Watson shared on social media, "It is necessary to set limits on what you will attempt to do, and choose to intentionally drop the ball in areas that matter less. Create boundaries on your time. No one else is going to do this for you. They will take as much as you are willing to give and keep asking for more." See how that translates? You can continue to spend and spend and spend more energy

## Lesson #13: Set and Respect Limits and Boundaries

than you even have, because the more you do, the more people will expect you to. Without boundaries, people will take advantage of what you have to offer. As I type these words, I know just how hard it is to acknowledge this. I certainly don't believe that people will intentionally take advantage of givers (at least most won't), but I also personally know that it does happen. Too often.

Setting boundaries is important. It's necessary. Spend your energy very wisely, and as soon you begin to see it as a form of currency, maybe, just maybe, it will be easier for you to let go of perfection, say "good enough," set priorities and drop the rest, and say no.

During my leave, I was intentional about looking inward to see what limits and boundaries I needed to put into place and respect. While reflecting on this, I found it truly helpful to start by looking at my values and then asking myself if where my energy was going aligned with those. In my darkest moments, I noticed that all of my energy was going to my work, and although I absolutely value my work, I have many other values, such as my family and friends, my relationships, and my health. With this new lens, I was able to put things in place to ensure that my energy was aligned with all of my values, not just one of them. It was also truly helpful to have this way of thinking in order to help me stick to my limits and boundaries.

One of the first things I needed to do was get my work email off of my phone. I struggled with this at first and decided that I would keep it on there for the first week during the transition period. After that, it was gone, and it stayed like that even after I went back to work. When a little red circle with a number appears on my mail app, I know that it's my personal email. I can be intentional about when I want to check my work email after hours, and I am now therefore in control of it, instead of it being in control of me. At first, I was nervous, and it felt strange not to be so connected, but as time went on, I realized that it was okay. No one expected responses right away; that was a self-inflicted expectation.

Setting a new email boundary quickly led to examining which notifications came through on my phone. My notification center is pretty boring now. Unless you text or call me, nothing is going to show on my locked screen. Did you like or comment on my Facebook post? I won't have a clue until I choose to open that app again. Did you send me a direct message on X? I hope you're not holding your breath because I have no clue until, again, I go to that app. You saw a hilarious reel on Instagram that you sent my way? Thanks, I'll see it when I'm ready. The point is, I really tried to take control of this handy-dandy little tool of mine, instead of letting it control me.

Then came even harder work, like setting limits and boundaries around my time and interactions. Leaving school by 4:30 p.m. became a must, and I had to work on being okay with leaving what I didn't get to for another day. I practiced saying no to events I really didn't want to attend; just because I was able to attend didn't mean I had to. I created space between myself and people I realized were draining me more than anything. I stopped volunteering for every committee. I started saying things like, "I'd be happy to help you with this, but I am only available for these thirty minutes."

Setting and respecting limits and boundaries is once again another example of something deeply personal that has to work for you. It's okay to play around with it until you figure out what you need, and it's okay to change your mind. It's also okay for limits and boundaries to change over time. Start by examining your values, and notice if there are any discrepancies between those and where your energy is going. That was truly eye-opening for me and helped me see things more clearly. This gave me a path that was easier to follow when implementing new boundaries, and these being founded in my values gave me the ability to stick to them.

## #*PheMOMenal* reflections:

- What is one thing you are spending energy on that isn't worth the return? Let it go. Without apology. Without explanation.

- What are you going to do today, tomorrow, this week, and this month to invest your energy? Don't let yourself run dry. Take care of you.

- Energy is a form of currency. Are you spending more than you have or investing in places that will provide a worthwhile return?

- You have to set limits and boundaries, because otherwise people will continue taking and asking for more.

# *Lesson #14*
## Follow Your Passions

*You will never be able to escape from your heart. So it's better to listen to what it has to say.*

—PAULO COELHO, *THE ALCHEMIST*

**FOLLOWING YOUR PASSIONS IS AN EXCELLENT WAY TO INVEST IN YOURSELF.** If our energy is a form of currency, and there are certain things that drain our energy (for which we need to set limits and boundaries, as explained in the previous lesson), surely there has to be the opposite effect. When you reflect on what gets you excited, what gives you energy, and what you want to do even when you're exhausted, what do you think of? What can't you wait to learn more about, lean into, and work at, despite the fact that it might be hard because it's new? Answering these questions should give you a pretty clear idea of where your passions lie and what could be energy builders. Follow those.

When my boys were babies and I was home with them for a year after each of their births, I discovered that I was very passionate about mom-related things. For example, I started learning how to make fancy birthday cakes to bring joy to my boys on their special days. These cakes were by no means perfect, but the process of making them and seeing how excited the kids were when the cakes were finally revealed to them made it all so worth it, and my boys couldn't care less if the cakes were leaning a bit to the right or if the fondant had cracked. They knew that a lot of love went into making that cake, and that was special.

I also became increasingly passionate about breastfeeding. I had had a horrible experience after having my first son, and I didn't want anyone else to have to go through that. After my second was born, and I was able to successfully breastfeed him until he self-weaned at thirteen months, I took it upon myself to advocate for mothers everywhere while also normalizing breastfeeding. It wasn't uncommon for my oldest to grab a doll and breastfeed it beside me while I nursed his younger brother. The same happened when I had the twins, and some days, it seemed like we had breastfeeding parties.

Once I found out I was about to become a mom of four, three of whom were going to be in diapers, I started to research cloth diapering in order to save money. This quickly turned into another crazy passion with a community of moms who were incredible. Something else I did to save my sanity was learn more about babywearing, and there, too, I became passionate about learning everything I could about woven wraps, soft structured wraps, ring slings, and so much more. I would spend hours practicing different ways to wrap and try different carries with stuffed animals before my twins were born. I soon became almost like a celebrity when I went out because people would stop me to drool over my two adorable, tiny newborns, both wrapped up onto me.

## Lesson #14: Follow Your Passions

But times change, and so do passions. It's important to notice this so we can shift where our energy goes to ensure that we continue being energized instead of drained. It's okay to quit something that isn't serving you anymore, even if it's done gradually over time.

When I went back to work, I slowly, very slowly, stopped making cakes. Doing this didn't bring me joy anymore, and instead it became a task I just didn't have the energy for anymore. When it was a passion, I made the time, and it actually energized me, but eventually, it was too much. I had to learn to let go, and it was hard. But over time, I did.

The breastfeeding also stopped shortly after returning to work. My twins nursed until they were about fourteen months and then decided they were done. It really was a sad moment, but one I knew wouldn't last forever anyways. Although I still really enjoy supporting other moms through their breastfeeding journeys, I am not there anymore, so things have definitely shifted and changed.

I'm happy to report that none of my boys are still in diapers, so we don't need to use cloth diapers anymore, so that passion has also changed. Along with that, I don't have babies or even toddlers anymore who request "guggles" (for snuggles), as Brecken used to say when he wanted to be picked up and worn.

Slowly but surely, my passions changed as my life evolved. As my boys needed me less and less, it provided me more time to dive into new passions that were always kind of hiding within me. You see, when I finished my schooling to become a teacher, I immediately got a permanent position. This meant that I was eligible for maternity leave not long after starting my career. I ended up getting pregnant late that summer and worked from September to the end of April before having my oldest on May 17. Yes, you read that right—I didn't even work a full year as a teacher before having my first child, with whom I stayed home for one year afterward. I went back to work for about a year and a half, and then I was off again with my second child. Finally, when I headed back to work after that year's leave, I was already pregnant and ended up working four months before being off for yet another year.

Needless to say, in that time of going back and forth from leave and the classroom, I didn't have a consistent chunk of time to really dive into this burning passion for my profession I had deep within me. But that all changed at lightning speed once I was done growing my family.

The year I went back to work after my last maternity leave, I was ready to fully dive into my profession as an educator. I took a lot of new risks that year and started changing many things in my classroom. By June, I was ready to take the next step and took an incredible trip to San Diego to attend the summer institute at High Tech High, which changed everything for me. While there, I was overcome with a sense of excitement and empowerment because I was surrounded by like-minded educators. This was the spark to a new, deep passion!

I continued exploring this passion and learning everything I could about innovation in education. I joined Twitter (now known as X), got connected, and quickly found out firsthand the power of having a community of like-minded people who push and support you. I read *Learn Like a PIRATE* by Paul Solarz and *Teach Like a PIRATE* by Dave Burgess and was floored when these authors interacted with me on social media. I joined an online course based on George Couros's book *The Innovator's Mindset*, through which I started blogging. I discovered that this form of reflection not only helped me organize my thoughts and become a better teacher but also helped me extend my chosen family of educators who were doing the same. I also decided to become a mentor and have a student teacher join my classroom to finish her year-long practicum before graduating with her teaching degree. I was excited to see what this new opportunity was going to provide. I knew that having her around would force me to think more deeply about my approaches, practices, and teaching, but it would also provide more flexibility when it came to trying new things and taking risks. Needless to say, my plate was overflowing, but I loved every minute of it because I was completely energized by it. Following this passion enabled me to prove that I deserved to be part of a hand-picked staff that was going to open up a brand-new innovative school, which is where I continue to teach today.

I didn't know at that moment in time that passions could quite literally drive you. I didn't know then that making time to explore passions was a necessity that felt rather easy and refreshing as opposed to another overwhelming to-do item on the list.

Have you ever had that experience? One where you experience such joy and pride and realize that if you follow that energy, you will find the time, even make the time to dive into this very thing, to learn and to grow. That is passion.

It doesn't mean that it's always easy, but the challenges seem much more manageable and worth it when you are energized because you are following your passions.

## #PheMOMenal reflections:

- Where do your passions lie? How are you making time to dive into these?

- Are there passions that aren't serving you anymore that you might consider letting go of? Reflect on your current passions and ask yourself if these are still truly passions of yours or if you're holding onto them for others or holding on to something you feel you "should" be doing.

- Are there any new passions that you'd like to explore and see where they take you? How can you make time for these?

- Are there other tasks or responsibilities that you need to take care of that you're not excited about? Could you reward yourself for having done these by then diving into something passion related?

# Lesson #15

## Habits, Small Goals, and Big Results

> *Every action you take is a vote for the type of person you wish to become. No single instance will transform your beliefs, but as the votes build up, so does the evidence of your new identity.*
>
> —JAMES CLEAR, *ATOMIC HABITS*

**WHATEVER YOU WANT TO DO, START SMALL.** Trust me, you don't need to make gigantic goals to move forward. In fact, making an overwhelming goal can actually stop you from moving forward. "I'll start tomorrow" is a lie that mothers tell themselves all the time, according to Rachel Hollis, author of *Girl, Wash Your Face*. She continues by pushing us to think about our commitments and how we keep our word when we say we're going to do something . . . except when we give our word to ourselves. I don't know about you, but I will go to the moon and back and make myself sick in order to hold up my end of the deal when I've said I will do something for someone. In the same breath, however, I will dismiss and put to the side everything I told myself I would do for me. Rachel encourages us to start small in order to start creating new habits that help us keep our promises to ourselves.

Starting small is one of the strategies to habit building that James Clear explores in his book, *Atomic Habits*. He calls this the "two-minute rule," which essentially pushes us to break down habits into a ritual that can take less than two minutes. This will establish the habit of showing up every day, which you can then build off of. As he says, "The secret is to always stay below the point where it feels like work."

After I had quite the scare where my stress load manifested info physical symptoms and had me worried that I had MS and breast cancer, I decided to make a promise to myself to start running so that I could do a better job of taking care of my mental and physical health. My small, manageable goal was to run for ten minutes and not to miss two days in a row. Had I known about James's two-minute rule back then, my first step would have been to simply get my shoes on. However, even without that knowledge, I still kept it small. I didn't want to run a marathon, I didn't even want to run a 5k then, I just focused on my small, manageable goal. I only had to think ahead one day at a time. *Can I run tomorrow? No? Okay, better run today then.* Although I did sometimes skip more than two days in a row, because the goal was small and manageable, it was easy to pick it back up. Since that day, I can honestly say not only that I've been running consistently but also that these habits I established while working on my tiny goals have made it possible for me to make new and bigger goals that I never dreamed would be possible.

I have a very similar story about writing. I didn't just wake up one day and decide to tackle the goal of writing a book. It started out small, and it actually started even before my blogging days. Again, while following my passions that came along with having children, I needed an outlet to share all that was going on with my growing boys with friends and family. Mixing that need with a passion I had for writing, I decided to start writing monthly updates, which included pictures of my growing family. The small monthly goal of writing about new milestones quickly turned into beautiful keepsake books for my boys. As my passions changed, my love of writing then transferred over into my educational world, where I eventually set myself the small goal of publishing a blog every week. Some posts were terrible, but getting into the habit of writing consistently helped me become a better writer. Eventually, years later, these blog posts gave me the confidence to grapple a new and bigger goal: to write a whole book.

Stop telling yourself you are going to start tomorrow. Decide on a small goal today, and make a commitment to yourself to keep this promise. Eventually, this small goal that you've maintained will turn into a habit. This habit will show you that you can stick with small goals, which will end up making a huge difference over time. You will begin to rewire your brain to place importance on the word you give yourself, and not just the one you give to others. You will learn to reflect on what it is that you are telling yourself *and* others. You will understand that overfilling your plate takes away from the time you have to do what you told yourself you would do. You will learn that you can't do it all and that your goals should absolutely be a priority. I know that's easier said than done, and I will be the first to admit that this is something I struggle with all the time, but I also see how important it is for me to work on it. Just keep swimming!

One promise I made to myself that I already mentioned was to take care of my mental and physical health. I have not wavered in this promise since I made it, but the goals within it have changed. I used to rely strictly on running, which grew from running for ten minutes a day and not missing two days in a row to eventually training for my first half marathon. Through this process, I learned that I couldn't be as strong of a runner if I didn't also strength train, which made my goal evolve. I was still taking care of my mental and physical health but was now doing so by running and strength training. When depression set in, the only way I could move my body was through hot yoga, so I went months without running consistently but still maintained the promise I'd made to myself to move my body in order to take care of my mental and physical health. As I got better, I started running more again. Recently, I could feel myself slipping because I was getting bored with the same routines, and I needed something that offered more flexibility. I decided to create a digital fitness journal to track what I was doing. This included beautiful pages to track my workouts, my weight, and the distance I run. The most powerful page for me is the one where I color a square for every day that I move my body. A pink square means I ran, a blue one means I did some strength training, teal is a walk, dark purple is dynamic recovery, and light purple is yoga. The uncolored white squares mean I did nothing that day, but that's also okay

> To see all of the pages in color and to get a template link to personalize your own fitness journal, head over to annickrauch.ca.

and necessary. I feel this is a beautiful example of James Clear's message that we should "reduce the scope, but stick to the schedule." In his blog post, "3 Time Management Tips That Actually Work," he goes on to explain that if our intention was to run three miles, but that time got away from us and we were left with only twenty minutes to work out, we could choose to change the schedule and therefore not work out, or we could alter the scope and run one mile, or do five sprints, or even thirty jumping jacks.

# Lesson #15: Habits, Small Goals, and Big Results

On a daily basis, the impact of doing five sprints isn't that significant, especially when you had planned to run 3 miles. But the cumulative impact of always staying on schedule is huge. No matter what the circumstance and no matter how small the workout, you know you're going to finish today's task. That's how little goals become lifetime habits. Finish something today, even if the scope is smaller than you anticipated.

I also love how James drives this home in *Atomic Habits* when he addresses one of the most common questions he hears: "How *long* does it take to build a new habit?" He reframes this by stating that a more accurate question is "How *many* does it take to form a new habit?" That is, how many repetitions does it take? If we look at it this way, it makes it pretty clear that consistency and sticking to the schedule can be much more powerful than skipping a day altogether.

My ongoing promise to myself is to move my body in order to take care of my mental and physical health. I am consistently doing that, but within that consistency, there's flexibility. If I'm mentally exhausted from a long day at work, maybe it's a yoga night. If we have four ice times and a basketball game on a weekday evening, maybe I will hop on the treadmill at work over lunch, or maybe it'll be a white square day. If the wind is howling outside and I really don't feel like I can mentally handle that on a run that day, maybe I will do some strength training in my basement instead. If I've had a particularly stressful day at work, I might head out for a run to clear my head. I have options, and within those, I maintain the schedule and alter the scope, but more importantly, I continue to keep my promise to myself. This habit now established, I start my day by asking myself, "What will I do to move my body today?"

If you have made a promise to yourself, stick to your plan, even if it means that you reduce the outcome for that one day. It's better to stick with a schedule than to leave it to the side completely. Small wins are still wins, and they reinforce the habit you are trying to create. They keep the promise you've made to yourself, and you continue to grow instead of being stagnant and risking falling off the wagon.

The process is simple: Make a goal, and don't let yourself break the promises you made to yourself. If you need to change the scope, go for it, but maintain the schedule.

Don't wait until tomorrow. What small goal can you make for yourself today? Get after it!

## #PheMOMenal reflections:

- What goals do you have? Can you break up this goal into smaller, more achievable ones as you continue to grow habits that will ultimately lead to you achieving your bigger goal and then some?

- Brainstorm challenges you might encounter while working toward your goal. How will you handle these? Make a plan for how your scope might change but how you can still maintain the schedule regardless.

# Lesson #16

## You Are Great, Own It

*You alone are enough. You have
nothing to prove to anybody.*

—MAYA ANGELOU

**OWNING YOUR GREATNESS IS AN UNDERRATED SKILL.** It's so important to give yourself the credit you deserve. Naturally, there's a difference between being arrogant and being humble, but striving for our best, being proud of our strengths, and sharing our journey to success shouldn't be something we hide.

I love how Dave Burgess speaks of the awkward question in his book, *Teach Like a PIRATE*.

> Do you want to be great?
>
> When I ask this question in my workshops, it is most often met with awkward silence, nervous shifting in the seats, and avoidance of eye contact.
>
> Why is it such an uncomfortable question for teachers to answer? We admire athletes who want to be great. In fact, we get annoyed and disappointed with athletes who don't have the drive to fulfill their potential. Yet, it is so

hard for most teachers to admit aloud that they want to be great.

This is a struggle for me, as I tend to downplay my accomplishments, and I know I'm not alone. Don't get me wrong, I absolutely want to be great and strive to always be learning, growing, and getting better than I was yesterday, but saying that out loud is hard! The fear of being perceived as someone who thinks they're better than others is real, but what if it had nothing to do with anyone else? What if success was simply measured against yourself? Then would it be easier to be proud of your greatness? Would it be easier to share all the work that goes on behind the scenes? Would it be easier to say things like, "Yes, I got this job because I've been working really hard and proved that I deserved it" instead of saying, "Yeah, I got super lucky."

We can look to our students and our children as examples here. Kids are seriously the best at this.

One day, I was saying goodbye to students as they were heading home at the end of the school day, and one of my former students walked by. I said, "Hey buddy, you've gotten really good at skating! I saw your mom's video on Instagram the other day!" He proceeded to say very nonchalantly, "I know."

Later on, my oldest son and I were at his appointment with a new specialist. As the doctor, whom he had never met before, was checking him over, she asked him if he played hockey. They chatted a bit, and then she asked, "Are you good?" to which he replied honestly after being caught off guard, "Uhhh . . . yes!"

My former student and my son were able to do what so many of us can't. They proudly acknowledged their growth and strengths and didn't have a care in the world how their abilities compared to others'. They were good in their own eyes, and that's all that mattered. Pretty amazing, if you ask me!

This tweet by educator and author Carly Spina hits the nail on the head:

Don't downplay your impact, your work. Did you make a tweak to a lesson to support a student? Did you reflect on an assessment & change something to make it more clear? Every win is a big win. Your work matters & makes an impact. Celebrate it. You're doing amazing things.

Unfortunately, it doesn't stop at downplaying our accomplishments. Something else that happens far too often is deflection. Don't get me wrong—it's important to acknowledge those who have helped us along the way, but at some point, we have to own our victories, too!

As I explained in "It Takes a Village," I wholeheartedly believe that people make all the difference. If you surround yourself with people who encourage you and understand your dreams, who push and support you to new heights, and who are there to pick you up when you fall (because you will), you will certainly grow more than if you try to do it alone. I hope that others will inspire you and will teach you things that you wouldn't have learned without them. The right people will create the conditions in which you will thrive. But who chooses the people you surround yourself with? Who takes the time to build those relationships with these crucial people in your life? Who cuts people out when they just bring you down?

You do.

I'm not much of a believer in luck. I believe that we create our own realities. Whether you want to believe that or not is up to you. But I do want you to consider how much *you* are creating your own successes. You should absolutely give credit to people who help you along the way, but don't forget that *you* do the work, and you deserve a lot of credit, too. You make the choices to learn and grow. You take risks and try and try again when you come up short. You silence your fears when they try to tell you that you can't do this. You—that's all you. And you are amazing!

What would happen if the next time someone complimented you, you simply said, "Thank you, I've been working hard on this!" What would happen if we owned our impact and celebrated not only the final product but the path it took to get there, too? What would happen if we celebrated others and acknowledged all of their efforts and impact, too? Still struggling with this idea? In *Teach Like a PIRATE*, Dave Burgess writes, "Your greatness in the classroom doesn't negatively impact or inhibit anyone else's opportunity to be great . . . your greatness only enhances the opportunities and possibilities for others. By being great, you are raising the bar and providing a model for others to emulate."

Knowing that your greatness would positively impact those you serve as well as your school community might just be the reframing you need to help you move past the idea that pursuing greatness is arrogant, selfish, or egotistical. By feeding your greatness, you are in turn feeding others'!

As Amber Teamann and Melinda Miller say in *Lead with Appreciation*, "Be loud when you're proud!"

You are great. Own it.

## #PheMOMenal reflections:

- What are your strengths? What can you celebrate today? What accomplishments are you proud of?
- How might you also highlight others' strengths and talents?
- Your greatness doesn't take away from others' greatness—it actually helps them. You being great is a gift to others. Go be great!

# Lesson #17
## Stop the Comparison—It's a Trap

*Comparison is the crush of conformity from one side and competition from the other—it's trying to simultaneously fit in and stand out. Comparison says, "Be like everyone else, but better."*

—BRENÉ BROWN, *ATLAS OF THE HEART*

**COMPARISON ISN'T VERY PRODUCTIVE.** Rather, it's important to look inward and reflect on our current circumstances to measure our successes. Although sometimes comparison can lead to positives, it often leads to negatives instead. Yes, through comparison, you might see things from a new perspective or feel inspired and motivated, but more often than not, you'll be left feeling like your feelings aren't valid or like you're not good enough.

At the very beginning of the pandemic, when we were on the heels of schools closing and I was sitting in the unknown while feeling the immense weight of virtually teaching my students and also supporting my four children who would be learning from home simultaneously, I came across this quote: "Your grandparents were called to war. You're being called to sit on your couch. You can do this."

Although I do think that keeping things in perspective is important, this quote rubbed me the wrong way. Why? Because I felt like it was dismissing my feelings around the pandemic. Sure, things could be worse, much worse; I could be called to war like my grandpa had been. However, my struggles in that moment were still completely valid. I felt like this quote was telling me to "suck it up" and that I should stop complaining about hard and very real things that were happening in my life at that very moment. This is something that I notice happens often. You've probably heard it, too: "I'm sorry, I really shouldn't be complaining about this to you. You are going through a lot, and this is nothing in comparison." But does your hard make theirs any less?

Another comparison trap to consider is that we are often comparing our reality to a curated, perfect one, which isn't real. What you see and use as a benchmark in your comparison is illusory. You then end up making yourself feel bad, or like you're not holding up, when the reality is that neither is the other person you were comparing yourself to.

Comparison, unfortunately, doesn't only happen between ourselves and others. It often happens between former versions of ourselves and our present selves. Raise your hand if you've compared your current body to your pre-pregnancy one. All of you? (Oh, except maybe the few men reading this.) Yeah, I thought so! You know how we have these memories that pop up on social media nowadays? Well, thanks to embarrassing super old Facebook statuses, each year I see a post I made that reads, "Pre-pregnancy weight definitely doesn't mean pre-pregnancy body!" Case in point.

Most of you probably already know Marie Kondo, but for those of you who don't, she's the "tidying expert," a bestselling author, and the star of the Netflix show *Tidying Up with Marie Kondo*. Her website introduces her this way: "Enchanted with organizing since her childhood, Marie began her tidying consultant business as a nineteen-year-old university student in Tokyo. Today, Marie is a renowned tidying expert helping people around the world to transform their cluttered homes into spaces of serenity and inspiration."

Still not ringing a bell? She is the one who asks her clients to hold items and answer the question "Does this bring you joy?" to help them determine if they should keep something or not.

Why am I talking about Marie Kondo and organization and tidying? Well, first of all, because it's my jam, but really, it's because recently, after having her third child, she learned a lesson that went viral. She said to the *Washington Post*, "Up until now, I was a professional tidier, so I did my best to keep my home tidy at all times. I have kind of given up on that in a good way for me. Now I realize what is important to me is enjoying spending time with my children at home."

Marie Kondo, the leading expert in organizing and tidying, has given up on it? Mic drop. She was humbled by her own kids and realized what is truly important in life, and having an immaculately tidy and organized home was not it. She's not comparing herself to her pre-children self and trying to match that life. Instead, she has learned to let go of things as her values shifted toward her children and family life instead of having a perfectly organized and Pinterest-worthy house. Different isn't bad—different is necessary. And as Theodore Roosevelt famously said, "Comparison is the thief of joy."

This is important to consider while dealing with challenges and adversity, too. When I was living with depression, it did me no good to compare my current self to my previous self. Same goes for when I sprained my ankle on a run and had to take some time off to heal. And it's no different than trying to compare my current weight as an avid runner to what I used to weigh when I wasn't exercising regularly. What's important is simply doing my best in my current circumstance, which is going to change from day to day. Getting out of bed and getting my boys to school when I was depressed was enough. Doing my physio exercises after I sprained my ankle to help me get back to running was my best at that time. Little things like having a cold, not getting enough sleep, or life-altering changes like having children or losing a loved one all impact what our best will look like. This isn't an excuse, it's a reminder that expecting ourselves to be able to accomplish what we did the day before when our circumstances were different isn't healthy. Don't compare—just do your best, your best in this very moment.

    Comparison isn't always necessarily bad. Like I said, if you're using it for perspective, then it can be helpful. I also often look to others for inspiration, motivation, and encouragement. That is also an example of how comparison could be positive. However, it's a very slippery slope because often comparison makes us feel bad or less than someone else, which might make us become overly competitive. It's more important to look inward and do something because it aligns with our passions and values, as opposed to looking outward and wanting to do something because someone else is doing it and we want to keep up. Stopping the tendency to compare is hard, but noticing it is the first step. I also find it helpful to try to understand where that need to compare is coming from. Is it jealousy? Insecurity? Practicing gratitude and reminding yourself of your strength while celebrating others goes a long way. I always make sure that those around me know what I appreciate and value about them. This, in turn, often creates reciprocity, where those same people make sure I know what strengths they see in me and what I bring to the table. Just like you cannot get taller by stepping on someone else, comparison isn't the way to growth. Kindness, support, encouragement, and grace are all better alternatives to comparison.

## #PheMOMenal reflections:

- ♥ The last lesson was about being great. Although this is still important, it's crucial to look inward to measure this and not compare yourself to others.

- ♥ When you notice yourself getting caught up in the comparison trap, whether it be with others or yourself, remind yourself that this is not helpful and look at your current reality instead.

- ♥ Practice gratitude and celebrate others. This will create reciprocity.

# Lesson #18

## Remember the Good

*Being positive does not mean ignoring the negative.
Being positive means overcoming the negative.
There is a big difference between the two.*

—MARC AND ANGEL, FROM *MARC AND ANGEL HACK LIFE*

**NO MATTER THE SITUATION, WE CAN ALWAYS FIND AT LEAST A TINY BIT OF POSITIVITY.** I'm not talking about toxic, excessive positivity, I'm more so talking about being intentional about looking for the good even when we're only seeing the bad. Sometimes, focusing on the good not only leads to us finding even more positives, it also helps us get through the harder stuff.

There was a period in my life where there was a lot of ugliness caused by conflict with neighbors that my family and I couldn't escape (but it is worth mentioning that this conflict has since been resolved). The stress it created for over a year was almost unbearable, and it left me feeling like a terrible mother. I was always on edge and couldn't exhale in my home and yard, places that should be a safe haven but couldn't be at the time. Camping was an important escape, especially during that time, as it provided a break from carrying that stress day in and day out.

During one particular camping trip during that stretch, my family and I headed to Falcon Lake, one of our favorite destinations. Although we didn't get one of our usual campsites, we were just lucky to get a spot at all that long weekend. As we got there on Friday and started setting up, we quickly realized that our spot wasn't private at all and that we were essentially sharing a space with three other families. We still enjoyed an amazing getaway and did all of our favorite activities—beach time, kayaking and paddleboarding, biking, ice cream trips, runs, campfires and s'mores, fishing, stick carving, and so much more.

One of my favorite memories from this trip was when the boys made breakfast, almost on their own. They'd been super interested in cooking and baking that summer, so we each gave them a job and then devoured this feast together. Emmett made the eggs, Brooks made sausage, Brecken made hash browns, and Caden (who has mastered making us burgers on the BBQ and had already made us several meals himself) was happy to get the easy job of making toast.

This camping trip also marked a bit of a milestone for our family, as our boys were actually interested in sitting around the fire for more than a few minutes and talking. Another thing they've been into lately

is "Would you rather . . . ," so this topic quickly overtook our conversation. We went around the circle and asked our "Would you rather . . . " questions and had fun listening to everyone's answers and reasoning.

*Would you rather swim in a pool full of pickle juice or mustard?*

*Would you rather live in the world of Minecraft or Fortnite?*

*Would you rather it always be winter or summer?*

*Would you rather be a famous YouTuber or an NHL player?*

As we were packing up to come home, one of our camping neighbors popped her head in and said, "I just wanted to let you know how much I enjoyed listening to your family and watching you interact this weekend. I have three boys who are now grown, and this brought back memories we made together when they were younger." We thanked her and responded that we didn't know if our boys were too loud or rambunctious, but she assured us that they were perfect and that if anyone was too loud or rambunctious, it was her boys when they were younger. She continued on to say that they grow up so fast and that she now has nine grandchildren.

This thirty-second interaction meant everything, especially considering the stress we were experiencing at the time due to the conflict with our neighbors back home. This perfect stranger, in the span of less than a minute, reminded me that I am a great mother, that my boys are wonderful, and that I'm doing all right. I want to hold onto that positive forever.

How quick are we to hold on to the bad? The negative tends to get stuck in our minds and is replayed over and over again. The positive, though, tends to be diminished and forgotten. However, no matter what you're going through, I assure you that there is always at least a sliver of positivity that can be found in any circumstance.

One weekend just before the pandemic hit, I was sitting in my hotel room in Fargo during a family vacation for my oldest son's hockey tournament, and I opened up the DBC Sunday Seven (a weekly email sent to subscribers, which includes seven little golden nuggets from the Dave Burgess Consulting Inc. crew). As I was reading through it, I thought to myself, *I bet I could come up with my own version of Sunday Seven with everything that has gone wrong already during this trip.* For fun, here it is.

1. Brecken fell asleep in the car while we were shopping. When we got to Scheels and he woke up to come out, his car seat was soaked because he had had an accident. That's fun when you're traveling by car!
2. Brooks had been under the weather for a while. My husband took him to the walk-in clinic before our trip to have someone check him over, but he was fine. Since he was still complaining of a sore throat, we gave him new medicine. He wasn't expecting the different taste and spit it out all over his jacket and down his shirt. This also happened right before going into Scheels. Needless to say, we simply drove right back to the hotel to regroup and clean up!
3. Once back at the hotel, I got a gut-wrenching text from my brother saying he and his wife had miscarried at sixteen weeks. This brought back a flood of emotions from my miscarriage, along with extreme heartache for them.
4. Early the next morning, I got a phone call from my old principal. I knew if she was calling, it was bad, and it was. I found out that morning that my former student Matthew had passed away. No words, just more heartbreak and unsuccessfully fighting back tears.
5. Brooks still wasn't any better and was now feverish, so I took him to the walk-in clinic. Bam. Double ear infection and strep throat.
6. I can't go into detail about number six, but the very short version is that Brooks got attacked by the older brother of a teammate, and another child stepped in to defend him. This child ended up taking a punch that was intended for Brooks. To say that this broke my heart and made my stress level skyrocket would be an understatement.

7. I got woken up around 11:45 p.m. that Saturday night to Brecken puking in his cot . . . and then again at 4:00 a.m. I can't make this stuff up.

There's my Sunday Seven of the Rauch family's misfortune during our trip to Fargo! It literally took everything in me not to break down. I had no space and no privacy to let it out, which was probably a blessing in disguise. I would have fallen apart.

But the positive I found? When I was *in* it, it was hard to find anything at all, but I actually said out loud at some point, "Brecken had red Gatorade and pizza for dinner, and blueberries for snack before bed, so at least his bright-pink puke smelled somewhat decent! And at least his puke didn't spill out of his top bunk cot and onto his twin brother." Yes, that was the positive I was holding on to. Not one but two positives! About bodily fluids, at that!

Once that trip was over and I'd had a bit of distance, there were so many more positives than just the half-decent-smelling barf! The group of parents and their kids from that trip were so wonderful and offered us so much love, support, and help through it all. Our four boys had the best time and weren't affected by the harder moments. Even Brooks perked right up with meds and holds a special place in his heart for two older boys who took him under their wings this trip. And despite the fact that Caden only won one of his games—the one I missed because I was in the hotel room with sick twins (I may or may not have cried when my husband jokingly texted me, saying I was banned from attending playoff games—I had had a rough few days, okay?), the team was in good spirits and had a blast through it all, as did the parents!

Sometimes it's hard to find the positives, but it's so helpful to stretch yourself and find even the smallest of things, even if it's gratitude for sweet-smelling pink puke! It might just help you overcome the negative.

So, I invite you to hold on to the good. Keep a feel-good folder in your inbox for when you receive a kind message from parents, students, colleagues, or admin. Have a physical folder or designated spot where you keep mementos that remind you of the good you're doing. Write in a gratitude journal. Be intentional about finding the positives, no matter how small. Refer to these often, and keep them fresh in your mind. Don't let them be diminished or forgotten.

What good can you remind yourself of and hold on to?

## PheMOMenal reflections:

- ♥ How can you document the little good things that happen so you can refer to them as needed?

- ♥ Might you consider having a feel-good folder in your email or in your filing cabinet at work? Perhaps a drawer in your nightstand could be a space to keep special mementos, notes or drawings made by your kids, or a journal to write little moments that would otherwise be forgotten over time.

# Lesson #19

## Small Actions, Big Impact

*A compliment is verbal sunshine.*

—ROBERT ORBEN

**BEING VALUED AND FEELING VALUED ARE TWO VERY DIFFERENT THINGS.**

Do the people that you value in your life know it? Do they feel valued?

I invite you to be the good for others, just as others provide sunshine for you. You never know how profound of an impact you might have on someone with a few kind words. Offer these freely and frequently.

Small actions can have a big impact.

During spring break 2020, in the middle of the pandemic, my boys and I set out to shower a few people with love by making sure that they knew just how valued they were. We wanted to go beyond simply internally appreciating them and instead *show* them. We wanted them to know, directly from us, that we appreciated all that they were doing.

First, we knew we wanted to support a local business, and we love donuts from a little shop called Bronuts, so we started there! We contacted them to make sure they could accommodate us by providing

## Lesson #19: Small Actions, Big Impact    117

curbside pickup (so my boys and I didn't have to go into the store) and asked if they could pack our donuts in individual bags (so that we wouldn't have to handle them and could safely hand them out). They agreed, and we hit the ground running! So exciting!

Then, we came up with a play on words and made cards that read: *We DONUT want you to forget how appreciated you are. Thank you for providing an essential service during these challenging times.*

Our family watched a simple Art Hub for Kids YouTube video to learn to draw a donut, and we completed our cards.

The next morning, we packed our cards and headed to Bronuts to pick up our order. On our drive there, we continued discussing who we might surprise with our sweet treats. This led to great conversations with my boys because at first they wanted to surprise their friends or our neighbors. Usually, this would be a great place to start, but on this day, we had a specific purpose to bring joy to people who were providing an essential service.

By the time we got to the shop, my boys had several ideas of who they might choose. We paid for the donuts, and with the most incredible smell filling our car, we drove around looking for deserving people.

First, Brecken spotted a police car! "There, Maman!" My oldest son had the idea of pulling up to their car at a red light and asking them to pull over—and that's just what we did. After a quick honk and rolling our windows down, we explained that we were doing random acts of kindness and that we had something for them to show our appreciation. We asked if they had a minute to pull over. It was kind of fun to pull over cops.

Next, Brooks wanted to make sure that his optometrist felt loved. This was a very special choice for him because the week prior he had broken his glasses while playing with his brothers. With everyone self-isolating and businesses either shutting down or limiting the people they could serve, our kind doctor not only fixed Brooks' glasses but also picked them up from our doorstep and then dropped them off afterward.

Emmett chose to surprise firefighters. We pulled up to a fire hall and knocked on the door. The man's smile was so bright, and Emmett was thrilled to see their dog.

Caden chose to surprise a worker at the McDonald's drive-thru. To him, this represented everyone who works in restaurants and helps to give ready-to-eat food to people who either don't have time to cook or are too tired to.

Next was my choice. We pulled up to Sobeys, our community grocery store, and I ran in and gave my card and donut to the lovely young lady who was wiping down and sanitizing the carts. I can't tell you how many times I've thought about how grateful I am that we were still able to go out and buy groceries. I don't even want to think about what would happen if this essential service were taken away.

Our sixth card and final donut was a special one for our dear neighbor who had been working ridiculously long hours as a nurse in the hospital. When we got home, she was at work, but we left it with her husband and sent her a text of what she could expect when she finally did get to go home later that day.

All and all, it was a terrific morning, and there's no doubt in my mind that our simple acts of kindness brought these people joy and also reminded them that they are seen and so very appreciated. I can only hope that we helped them *feel* valued instead of them simply *being* valued.

That distinction is important. But it doesn't always have to be so complicated. You don't need to make cards and deliver donuts to ensure people feel valued. In fact, you don't even need to make an elaborate plan or spend any money at all.

I was in class one day when a divisional employee from the learning team, Roy Norris, came into my room to help with assessments. Although I had never met Roy before, I was connected with him on Twitter, and our paths had crossed once or twice. As he brought one student back to take the next, he noticed that my student teacher was teaching and came up to me to share the most incredible message. He said, "I just want you to know that I've read everything you've ever written. Keep writing!" I was floored. Weeks before this interaction, I had signed the contact to write this book but hadn't announced it. He didn't know that I was working on a book; my blog posts had simply had an impact on him, and he made sure I knew it. In that moment, Roy shared the good, and I can't tell you how much I appreciated it and needed it. That simple statement that he chose to share with me gave me the boost in confidence I needed to keep writing . . . a whole book.

What can you do today to share the good and make sure that those around you feel valued? This lesson is very similar to the one about help, in that if you share the good, it will fill you up just as much as it fills up the receiver. You might also consider noting when people do things for you that make you feel valued. Add those notes to your feel-good folder and refer to them often.

Roy, thank you for making sure I knew that my words had impacted you and encouraging me to keep going. Your kind words meant everything to me that day.

## #PheMOMenal reflections:

- Small actions and sharing positive words can have an immense impact on others, one you might never realize.

- How might you consider making sure those around you feel valued?

- Random acts of kindness don't have to be elaborate to have a great impact. Consider buying a colleague a coffee, writing a heartfelt note, or simply sharing a kind word of appreciation. You will notice that this fills you up just as much as it does them!

# Lesson #20

## You ARE Making a Difference

*Our fingerprints don't fade from the lives we touch.*
—JUDY BLUME

**YOU ARE IN THE HEART-WORK BUSINESS.** You may not realize it, but the little things you do each day make so much difference.

As a teacher and a mom, I get to experience this from both sides.

When Brooks was six, he started complaining about "barfing a little in his mouth and swallowing it." We contacted the doctor who's been following him since his surgery at birth, who sent him for an X-ray. This test wasn't conclusive, so she decided to send him for an imaging study of the esophagus, stomach, and duodenum. This entailed Brooks fasting for eight hours before the appointment and then him drinking a special vanilla-flavored, thick-ish white liquid while the doctor watched and took pictures of it making its way through his body.

Brooks was an all-star. He was bubbly and talkative, chugged back the liquid, leaving behind the cutest white mustache above his lip, and loved watching the screen as he saw the liquid bounce around inside his body. It was a hugely positive experience that could have been a complete nightmare.

Sure, I prepared him as best as I could before the appointment, talking calmly about what I thought might happen. I played it up, saying that not only would he get to miss a day of school but I would, too, and that we'd make a special day out of it. Having said that, I'm not the one who made this experience so positive. I bet you can guess who did.

The nurses. The technicians. The doctor. They are in the heart-work business.

As soon as Brooks was called in for his appointment, a sweet woman talked and engaged with him while we walked down the hall and into the room. She told him about the white liquid that was kind of like a milkshake but not cold. She asked him if he was hungry and what he was going to eat once he was done with his appointment: "Oh, a bagel with Nutella? Have you ever tried peanut butter AND Nutella?" This type of conversation continued with the other people involved in his procedure. Despite the fact that they didn't know my son, they took these precious minutes to build a relationship with him before they got to the "here's what we need you to do for the doctor" part. You could tell that he was over-the-moon with all of the attention he was getting and was comfortable with the team caring for him. They showed him the equipment and explained to him what he was seeing on the screen. They giggled with him and told him how well he was doing.

Be still, my heart.

As I was driving home with Brooks and thinking about all of these wonderful women who took such great care of my little boy, and how grateful I was for them going *above and beyond* and making this experience positive for him, I realized something. I, too, have created this same feeling for parents. I, too, am in the heart-work business. Perhaps the nurses, technicians, and doctors didn't go *above and beyond* but rather did what they always do, because it is in their nature. Maybe they understand that these interactions make all the difference. Maybe it brings them as much joy as it brings others.

I remember one day in particular, a student came to school feeling sad. When I checked in with her and asked how she was doing, she said with tears pooling in her eyes, "Not good. I didn't hug Mama this morning." I got down on my knee and whispered back, "It is hard to miss Mommy. What if we made Mommy a little video after the morning announcements. Would that help?" Instantly, her eyes lit up and her mood changed. Did I do this to go above and beyond? Of course not—it's second nature because I am in the heart-work business. I knew that until this student felt better, there wasn't much she'd be able to take in from the day. I knew that she needed love and a bit of time. "Hi, Mama. I forgot to give you a huggy. I just wanted to say I love you." A nine-second video. Mom responded, saying that they had all had a rough morning and that the video made her cry. She wrote, "Thank you so much! I can see why so many talk so highly of you. This truly made my day." I read part of her response to my student, who was already back to herself by then. It took thirty seconds out of my day but changed my student's and her mom's whole day.

I bet you don't think about it twice when you do the heart-work. Maybe you don't even notice when you do it. It probably has become an instinct for you. You do what is needed to show care and love. You build relationships, both with your students and their families. You do the heart-work. And I just want to remind you that it is appreciated and is making all of the difference.

Thank you for being in the heart-work business.

## #*PheMOMenal* reflections:

- ♥ Find a way to remind yourself of the good you're creating and the impact you're having. That way, you can refer back to it whenever you need to.

- I have a physical feel-good folder in my filing cabinet at school. This folder is filled with cards, pictures, and messages I've received over the years that remind me of the good.

- I have the same kind of folder in my email inbox for all the messages I want to look over when I'm having a particularly hard day or when self-doubt creeps in.

# Lesson #21

## Guilt:
### Feel It to Heal It

*Grace means that all of your mistakes now serve a purpose instead of serving shame.*

—BRENÉ BROWN

**GUILT IS A WORD THAT HAS COME UP MANY TIMES IN THE PREVIOUS LESSONS.** If you're a mom and a teacher, you've experienced guilt, no doubt about it. So, what do we do about all the guilt?

Often, when I am experiencing big emotions, I write about them. Sometimes these get published on my blog, and other times they stay tucked away just for me. Writing my feelings and acknowledging them is usually enough to help me lean in, learn, grow, and let them go to move past them. What has been striking, though, which really shouldn't come as a big surprise, is that my most vulnerable posts always resonate with many. But of course they would. Surely I can't be the only one feeling those things. Guilt is one of the big emotions that overwhelms me on the best of days, never mind the hard ones, and I know I'm not alone.

In *Innovate Inside the Box*, Katie Novak shares,

> My auntie Jan once told me, "Guilt is a useless emotion." So often, we look back on mistakes we have made with regret and guilt as opposed to determining the source of what went wrong and fixing it . . . We attend professional development and get nothing out of it and then feel guilty that we took a day away from our students, for what? Subpar coffee and brownies during a five-minute break? Our students all fail a test, or misbehave for the sub, and we feel guilty. Listen to my auntie Jan: Guilt is *useless*.

And in *Girl, Stop Apologizing,* Rachel Hollis writes,

> Mommy guilt, in case you haven't ever experienced it personally, is this gross, horrendous, cancerous thing that lodges itself in your heart and creeps its way to your head where it festers forever—unless you actively choose to kill it. Mommy guilt likes to remind you on the regular of all the ways you're failing your children. Some women struggle with guilt on topics like going to work. Others struggle under the weight of guilt associated with everything from wanting time for themselves to not feeding their kids the right kind of blueberries. And I guess, if that was the only thing you had to worry about, maybe it wouldn't be so bad, but being a mom means there are 967 things to worry about on any given day. So not only are you responsible for someone else's clothes and shelter and dental hygiene, but you're also going to go ahead and beat yourself up for those 967 choices you're making *as you're making them* and think that this will empower you to be better next time? No way. This is only going to confuse and overwhelm you and zap you of whatever confidence you had in yourself as a mom, which, let's be honest, is tenuous on the best of days.

One thing I wrote to myself one day was "And that guilt you are feeling? Let it go. It doesn't do you any good to hold on to it."

I know what you're thinking.

*Let it go? Ha! Everyone says that . . . easier said than done! HOW do I let it go?!*

Trust me, I get it! Guilt is one tough thing to feel and an even harder feeling to get rid of. I certainly haven't figured out how to let it go all of the time, but I've found that acknowledging the feeling does wonders.

In her book *Dodging Energy Vampires*, Christiane Northrup shares a pretty fantastic and brilliantly simple way to release guilt.

> Yes, putting yourself first can be hard—much harder said than done—but it's worth it. When you begin to do this, you will feel guilty—guaranteed. When that happens, you must notice the guilt and accept it. This alone takes away some of the power of guilt. I like to do a fun exercise whenever guilt pops up for me. As soon as I feel it, I fully and lovingly say to myself, "Nice going! You're nailing it! No one has ever done guilt better than you're doing it."
>
> Believe it or not, completely accepting your guilt will help you release it much faster than hanging on to it and beating yourself up for it. It is when we resist feeling what we're really feeling that we get stuck. As the saying goes, "You've got to feel it to heal it." And though guilt and shame are incredibly painful feelings, they're far better felt and released than left smoldering inside.

As teachers and moms, we are problem solvers. When we can't fix a problem, though, guilt starts to set in. And let's be real, there are a million problems that we cannot fix, be it a systematic problem, a budget issue, or something else out of our control. What do we do then? My therapist suggested one day that instead of burying those feelings I should acknowledge and validate them: "Of course it's normal to feel frustrated, angry, resentful, sad, etc. right now. Anyone going through this would be feeling this, too."

For me, writing about my feelings of guilt helps me to acknowledge them and let them go. But when I don't have time to do this, I have begun using that positive self-talk exercise where I acknowledge and validate what I am feeling. It's still an ongoing struggle, but I'm sure it always will be, so I will simply keep trying to get better every day.

## #PheMOMenal reflections:

- Acknowledge and validate big feelings in order to take some of their power away.
- Try saying, "Of course it's normal to feel overwhelmed, frustrated, angry, sad, etc. Anyone going through this would be feeling this, too."
- If you journal, write about your feelings in a nonjudgmental way.
- Just because big feelings surface, it doesn't mean they should overtake you.
- Feeling and releasing is better than holding and burying.

# Conclusion
## I'll Leave You with This

**THINGS ARE ALWAYS CHANGING.**

Of all the things I've learned through thirteen-plus years of teaching and being a mother, this is the one I find most important to remind myself of—often. Things are always changing.

Just when I think I have something figured out, everything changes, and I feel like I'm back to the start. Being flexible enough to adapt to the ever-changing ebb and flow of life is probably the most important skill to develop. Notice that I didn't say we need to seamlessly adapt or that the changes should never throw us for a loop. Rather, it's important to keep showing up, keep trying, keep getting back up after we fall, and to try and implement the lessons we've learned through all of the highs and lows.

I've fallen more times than I can count, and although I've shared many of these experiences throughout this book, know that this is only a tiny glimpse into my very chaotic, busy, and challenging life. I don't pretend to know everything, nor do I believe that the lessons I've learned are a cure-all. These are simply the lessons I have learned so far, that have helped me, and that I hope might be helpful for others. You, however, probably could add several chapters to this book. My hope is that this book is the start of a conversation, the founding of a community of mothers and educators who come together to support one another, to lift each other up, and to remind themselves and each other that we are great and we are capable of so much more than we even know. I also hope that this is the beginning of a conversation, one that includes an open dialogue about lessons we've learned and how these might benefit others in our reality. I still have so much to learn, and I hope that you will be part of the reason I continue to grow and be better, for myself, for my family, and for my students.

You are a mother. You are an educator. You are a woman. You are strong, capable, and worthy. You are not defined by your circumstances. You deserve to chase after your wildest dreams. You will strive to the greatest heights. And I, for one, cannot wait to see where you go.

Get after it, PheMOMenal Teacher!

# Bibliography

Apsey, Allyson. *Leading the Whole Teacher: Strategies for Supporting the Educators in Your School*. San Diego: Dave Burgess Consulting, 2022.

Art for Kids Hub. "How to Draw a Doughnut," June 9, 2017. https://www.youtube.com/watch?v=OaiT-PWTcig.

Bearden, Kim. *Talk to Me: Find the Right Words to Inspire, Encourage and Get Things Done*. San Diego: Dave Burgess Consulting, 2018.

Brown, Brené. *Daring Greatly: How the Courage to Be Vulnerable Transforms the Way We Live, Love, Parent and Lead. Bren Brown.* New York: Avery Publishing, 2012.

Burgess, Dave. *Teach Like a Pirate: Increase Student Engagement, Boost Your Creativity, and Transform Your Life as an Educator*. San Diego: Dave Burgess Consulting, 2012.

Cavey, Tim. "Teacher Wellness and Self-Care: How to Avoid Burnout and Rekindle Your Fire." March 24, 2021. Podcast 57:25. https://teachersonfire.net/2021/03/24/teacher-wellness-and-self-care-how-to-avoid-burnout-and-rekindle-your-fire/.

Clear, James. *Atomic Habits: An Easy and Proven Way to Build Good Habits and Break Bad Ones*. New York: Avery, 2018.

Clear, James. "3 Time Management Tips That Will Improve Your Health and Productivity." February 4, 2020. https://jamesclear.com/time-management-tips.

Couros, George, and Katie Novak. *Innovate Inside the Box: Empowering Learners through UDL and the Innovator's Mindset*. San Diego: IMPress, 2019.

CTF-FCE. *Blog Perspectives—CTF-FCE*. April 26, 2022. *CTF-FCE*. https://www.ctf-fce.ca/blog-perspectives/.

Doyle, Glennon. *Untamed*. New York: Dial Press, 2020.

"Government Must Act Now." The Manitoba Teachers' Society, January 6, 2021. www.mbteach.org/mtscms/2021/01/06/government-must-act-now/.

Hollis, Rachel. *Girl, Stop Apologizing: A Shame-Free Plan for Embracing and Achieving Your Goals*. New York: HarperCollins Leadership, 2019.

Hollis, Rachel. *Girl, Wash Your Face: Stop Believing the Lies about Who You Are So You Can Become Who You Were Meant to Be*. Nashville: Thomas Nelson, 2018.

Grant, Adam [@AdamMGrant]. X post. July 12, 2022, 10:07 AM. https://twitter.com/AdamMGrant/status/1546873796895723521?lang=en.

Koncius, Jura. "Marie Kondo's Life Is Messier Now—and She's Fine with It." *Washington Post*, January 28, 2023. https://www.washingtonpost.com/home/2023/01/26/marie-kondo-kurashi-inner-calm/.

KonMari Media, Inc. "About Marie Kondo—KonMari | The Official Website of Marie Kondo." February 3, 2022. https://konmari.com/about-marie-kondo/.

Maroutian, Emily. *Thirty: A Collection of Personal Quotes, Advice, and Lessons*. CreateSpace, 2015.

Northrup, Christiane. *Dodging Energy Vampires: An Empath's Guide to Evading Relationships That Drain You and Restoring Your Health and Power*. Carlsbad, CA: Hay House Inc., 2018.

Pharaon, Vienna [@mindfulmft]. Instagram post. June 20, 2018. https://www.instagram.com/p/BkQ3xFGgNE9/?utm_source=ig_share_sheet&igshid=2atykp70actl.

Tricarico, Dan. *The Zen Teacher: Creating Focus, Simplicity, and Tranquility in the Classroom*. San Diego: Dave Burgess Consulting, 2015.

Rowell, Lainie. *Evolving with Gratitude: Small Practices in Learning Communities That Make a Big Difference with Kids, Peers, and the World*. San Diego: IMPress, 2022.

Siegel, Daniel J. *The Developing Mind, Second Edition: How Relationships and the Brain Interact to Shape Who We Are*. New York: Guilford Publications, 2015.

Spina, Carly [@MrsSpinasClass]. X post. February 16, 2020, 9:43 AM. https://twitter.com/MrsSpinasClass/status/1229068816161869824?ref_src=twsrc%5Etfw.

Teamann, Amber, and Melinda Miller. *Lead with Appreciation: Fostering a Culture of Gratitude*. San Diego: Dave Burgess Consulting, 2019.

Watson, Angela. 2020. "I posted this in the 40 Hour Teacher Workweek groups and was asked to share it publicly, so here goes." Facebook, September 26, 2020.

# Acknowledgments

This book wouldn't have been possible without the love and support of my husband, Chris. Thank you for holding down the fort and giving me the time and space I needed to focus on this dream of mine. I couldn't do this life we've built without you. I love you.

To my sons, Caden, Emmett, Brooks, and Brecken, thank you not only for understanding that it is important for me to follow my dreams but also for teaching me so much along the way. Although I am the mom and the teacher, you've taught me more than I'd ever dreamed possible. You are a big part of the reason I was able to fill the pages of this book with lessons I've learned. Thank you for being incredible little teachers.

To my parents, I know I've said it before, but I will continue to say it. Thank you for the countless ways you support me and my family. Without your help watching the boys, especially during the times when I scheduled writer's retreats, this book wouldn't have come together. Maman, thanks also for reading my manuscript before I even submitted it and for giving me permission to share some of your journey.

Thank you to my siblings. It means a lot that you were all so interested and invested in my book-writing journey. Lisa, you were a constant source of encouragement, which kept me going on days that were harder. Dan, thanks for lending me your house for a weekend so I could write in peace. Jus, even though you're far away, it never feels like it. Thanks for your advice, especially when it came to titles. To my sister-in-law Paige, it's extra special to finally have another teacher in the family, and I always appreciate all the ways you understand my reality!

I am grateful to my friends and biggest cheerleaders, who were always just a text or a call away when I was doubting myself. Nycol, thanks for always asking for updates and never allowing me to downplay my accomplishments. Tamara, thanks for the early brainstorming sessions at the spa and holding my hand anytime I needed it. Tara, thank you for your guidance, validation, and wisdom. You are a gem! Hadera, thanks for your excitement and for talking all shades of pink with me.

Jen, thanks for always capturing the most beautiful family moments through your talent in photography. You and I have definitely created our very own memories over the last thirteen years, and I am glad you are part of this book journey!

I am incredibly grateful for something very rare that I am blessed to have: the Dream Team. To my same grade colleagues, Caelin, Makaela, Nadine, and student services support teacher Sheila, thank you for being such a huge source of support. You know me better than most when it comes to being a mom and a teacher, and I value your friendship beyond measure.

To my students past, present, and future, thank you for making this job I love so fun. It is an honor to watch you learn and grow every single day. To my students' families, thank you for trusting me with your little ones and giving me grace as I learn to be the best teacher I can be, while also being a great mom and not losing sight of myself.

To George Couros, thanks for pushing me to start blogging way back in 2016 and for your support since. Without your not-so-gentle nudges to write consistently, I would have never had the confidence to tackle writing a book.

To Sr. Jo-Ann and the Grey Nuns, thank you for giving me a space to escape to for a whole weekend so that I could focus solely on writing.

To Lindsey and the whole team at The Reading List, thank you from the bottom of my heart for all of your hard work in making this book all that it is. Through every single phrase, I continued to be amazed by how you brought this vision I had to life. You are all phenomenal.

Last but certainly not least, the biggest of thanks to Dave Burgess and Dave Burgess Consulting Inc. Dave, what you've created is so special, and I am a better teacher today because of you and your company. Thank you for believing in my message enough to take a chance on me. Ever since I joined the #tlap crew all these years ago, I knew I wanted to be part of it, and I am honored to now officially be in the family.

# About the Author

Annick Rauch is a passionate grade 1 French immersion teacher who began her teaching career in 2009. She was chosen as an inaugural educator to open École Sage Creek School where she continues to teach today. She prides herself on developing relationships with students in order to create a classroom community where everyone encourages, supports, and challenges one another. She incorporates students' interests and passions into their learning and truly loves what she does.

Outside of school, Annick is a very busy mom. She and her husband Chris have four energetic boys: Caden, Emmett, Brooks, and Brecken, who all play a variety of sports. They also have a silver lab named Ellie, who is thoroughly convinced she is the fifth child. Annick loves to go camping with her family, and she also makes it a priority to carve out time for trips with friends.

Although busy, Annick doesn't let that stop her from pursuing her dreams outside of her work and home life. She is an avid runner with several half marathons under her belt. She blogs at annickrauch.ca and is a frequent contributor and collaborator with the education community on social media. She is a lifelong learner who continues to follow her passions.

If you would like to bring the PheMOMenal Teacher message to your school, business, or event, connect with Annick on any platform below:

- @AnnickRauch
- @annickrauch
- annickrauch.ca
- annickrauch@gmail.com
- #PheMOMenal

# More from Dave Burgess Consulting, Inc.

Since 2012, DBCI has published books that inspire and equip educators to be their best. For more information on our titles or to purchase bulk orders for your school, district, or book study, visit DaveBurgessConsulting.com/DBCIbooks.

### More from the *Like a PIRATE*™ Series
*Teach Like a PIRATE* by Dave Burgess
*eXPlore Like a PIRATE* by Michael Matera
*Learn Like a PIRATE* by Paul Solarz
*Plan Like a PIRATE* by Dawn M. Harris
*Play Like a PIRATE* by Quinn Rollins
*Run Like a PIRATE* by Adam Welcome
*Tech Like a PIRATE* by Matt Miller

### Lead Like a PIRATE™ Series
*Lead Like a PIRATE* by Shelley Burgess and Beth Houf
*Balance Like a PIRATE* by Jessica Cabeen, Jessica Johnson, and Sarah Johnson
*Lead beyond Your Title* by Nili Bartley
*Lead with Appreciation* by Amber Teamann and Melinda Miller
*Lead with Collaboration* by Allyson Apsey and Jessica Gomez
*Lead with Culture* by Jay Billy
*Lead with Instructional Rounds* by Vicki Wilson
*Lead with Literacy* by Mandy Ellis
*She Leads* by Dr. Rachael George and Majalise W. Tolan

### Leadership & School Culture
*Beyond the Surface of Restorative Practices* by Marisol Rerucha
*Change the Narrative* by Henry J. Turner and Kathy Lopes
*Choosing to See* by Pamela Seda and Kyndall Brown

*Culturize* by Jimmy Casas
*Discipline Win* by Andy Jacks
*Escaping the School Leader's Dunk Tank* by Rebecca Coda and Rick Jetter
*Fight Song* by Kim Bearden
*From Teacher to Leader* by Starr Sackstein
*If the Dance Floor Is Empty, Change the Song* by Joe Clark
*The Innovator's Mindset* by George Couros
*It's OK to Say "They"* by Christy Whittlesey
*Kids Deserve It!* by Todd Nesloney and Adam Welcome
*Leading the Whole Teacher* by Allyson Apsey
*Let Them Speak* by Rebecca Coda and Rick Jetter
*The Limitless School* by Abe Hege and Adam Dovico
*Live Your Excellence* by Jimmy Casas
*Next-Level Teaching* by Jonathan Alsheimer
*The Pepper Effect* by Sean Gaillard
*Principaled* by Kate Barker, Kourtney Ferrua, and Rachael George
*The Principled Principal* by Jeffrey Zoul and Anthony McConnell
*Relentless* by Hamish Brewer
*The Secret Solution* by Todd Whitaker, Sam Miller, and Ryan Donlan
*Start. Right. Now.* by Todd Whitaker, Jeffrey Zoul, and Jimmy Casas
*Stop. Right. Now.* by Jimmy Casas and Jeffrey Zoul
*Teachers Deserve It* by Rae Hughart and Adam Welcome
*Teach Your Class Off* by CJ Reynolds
*They Call Me "Mr. De"* by Frank DeAngelis
*Thrive through the Five* by Jill M. Siler
*Unmapped Potential* by Julie Hasson and Missy Lennard
*When Kids Lead* by Todd Nesloney and Adam Dovico
*Word Shift* by Joy Kirr
*Your School Rocks* by Ryan McLane and Eric Lowe

**Technology & Tools**
*50 Things to Go Further with Google Classroom* by Alice Keeler and Libbi Miller
*50 Things You Can Do with Google Classroom* by Alice Keeler and Libbi Miller
*140 Twitter Tips for Educators* by Brad Currie, Billy Krakower, and Scott Rocco
*Block Breaker* by Brian Aspinall

*Building Blocks for Tiny Techies* by Jamila "Mia" Leonard
*Code Breaker* by Brian Aspinall
*The Complete EdTech Coach* by Katherine Goyette and Adam Juarez
*Control Alt Achieve* by Eric Curts
*The Esports Education Playbook* by Chris Aviles, Steve Isaacs, Christine Lion-Bailey, and Jesse Lubinsky
*Google Apps for Littles* by Christine Pinto and Alice Keeler
*Master the Media* by Julie Smith
*Raising Digital Leaders* by Jennifer Casa-Todd
*Reality Bytes* by Christine Lion-Bailey, Jesse Lubinsky, and Micah Shippee, PhD
*Sail the 7 Cs with Microsoft Education* by Becky Keene and Kathi Kersznowski
*Shake Up Learning* by Kasey Bell
*Social LEADia* by Jennifer Casa-Todd
*Stepping Up to Google Classroom* by Alice Keeler and Kimberly Mattina
*Teaching Math with Google Apps* by Alice Keeler and Diana Herrington
*Teachingland* by Amanda Fox and Mary Ellen Weeks
*Teaching with Google Jamboard* by Alice Keeler and Kimberly Mattina

**Teaching Methods & Materials**
*All 4s and 5s* by Andrew Sharos
*Boredom Busters* by Katie Powell
*The Classroom Chef* by John Stevens and Matt Vaudrey
*The Collaborative Classroom* by Trevor Muir
*Copyrighteous* by Diana Gill
*CREATE* by Bethany J. Petty
*Deploying EduProtocols* by Kim Voge, with Jon Corippo and Marlena Hebern
*Ditch That Homework* by Matt Miller and Alice Keeler
*Ditch That Textbook* by Matt Miller
*Don't Ditch That Tech* by Matt Miller, Nate Ridgway, and Angelia Ridgway
*EDrenaline Rush* by John Meehan
*Educated by Design* by Michael Cohen, The Tech Rabbi
*The EduProtocol Field Guide* by Marlena Hebern and Jon Corippo
*The EduProtocol Field Guide: Book 2* by Marlena Hebern and Jon Corippo
*The EduProtocol Field Guide: Math Edition* by Lisa Nowakowski and Jeremiah Ruesch

*The EduProtocol Field Guide: Social Studies Edition* by Dr. Scott M. Petri and Adam Moler
*Empowered to Choose: A Practical Guide to Personalized Learning* by Andrew Easton
*Expedition Science* by Becky Schnekser
*Frustration Busters* by Katie Powell
*Fully Engaged* by Michael Matera and John Meehan
*Game On? Brain On!* by Lindsay Portnoy, PhD
*Guided Math AMPED* by Reagan Tunstall
*Innovating Play* by Jessica LaBar-Twomy and Christine Pinto
*Instructional Coaching Connection* by Nathan Lang-Raad
*Instant Relevance* by Denis Sheeran
*Keeping the Wonder* by Jenna Copper, Ashley Bible, Abby Gross, and Staci Lamb
*LAUNCH* by John Spencer and A.J. Juliani
*Learning in the Zone* by Dr. Sonny Magana
*Lights, Cameras, TEACH!* by Kevin J. Butler
*Make Learning MAGICAL* by Tisha Richmond
*Pass the Baton* by Kathryn Finch and Theresa Hoover
*Project-Based Learning Anywhere* by Lori Elliott
*Pure Genius* by Don Wettrick
*The Revolution* by Darren Ellwein and Derek McCoy
*The Science Box* by Kim Adsit and Adam Peterson
*Shift This!* by Joy Kirr
*Skyrocket Your Teacher Coaching* by Michael Cary Sonbert
*Spark Learning* by Ramsey Musallam
*Sparks in the Dark* by Travis Crowder and Todd Nesloney
*Table Talk Math* by John Stevens
*Unpack Your Impact* by Naomi O'Brien and LaNesha Tabb
*The Wild Card* by Hope and Wade King
*Writefully Empowered* by Jacob Chastain
*The Writing on the Classroom Wall* by Steve Wyborney
*You Are Poetry* by Mike Johnston
*You'll Never Guess What I'm Thinking About* by Naomi O'Brien

**Inspiration, Professional Growth & Personal Development**
*Be REAL* by Tara Martin
*Be the One for Kids* by Ryan Sheehy

## More from Dave Burgess Consulting, Inc.

*The Coach ADVenture* by Amy Illingworth
*Creatively Productive* by Lisa Johnson
*Educational Eye Exam* by Alicia Ray
*The EduNinja Mindset* by Jennifer Burdis
*Empower Our Girls* by Lynmara Colón and Adam Welcome
*Finding Lifelines* by Andrew Grieve and Andrew Sharos
*The Four O'Clock Faculty* by Rich Czyz
*How Much Water Do We Have?* by Pete and Kris Nunweiler
*P Is for Pirate* by Dave and Shelley Burgess
*A Passion for Kindness* by Tamara Letter
*The Path to Serendipity* by Allyson Apsey
*Recipes for Resilience* by Robert A. Martinez
*Rogue Leader* by Rich Czyz
*Sanctuaries* by Dan Tricarico
*Saving Sycamore* by Molly B. Hudgens
*The Secret Sauce* by Rich Czyz
*Shattering the Perfect Teacher Myth* by Aaron Hogan
*Stories from Webb* by Todd Nesloney
*Talk to Me* by Kim Bearden
*Teach Better* by Chad Ostrowski, Tiffany Ott, Rae Hughart, and Jeff Gargas
*Teach Me, Teacher* by Jacob Chastain
*Teach, Play, Learn!* by Adam Peterson
*The Teachers of Oz* by Herbie Raad and Nathan Lang-Raad
*TeamMakers* by Laura Robb and Evan Robb
*Through the Lens of Serendipity* by Allyson Apsey
*The Zen Teacher* by Dan Tricarico
*Write Here and Now* by Dan Tricarico

### Children's Books
*The Adventures of Little Mickey* by Mickey Smith Jr.
*Alpert* by LaNesha Tabb
*Alpert & Friends* by LaNesha Tabb
*Beyond Us* by Aaron Polansky
*Cannonball In* by Tara Martin
*Dolphins in Trees* by Aaron Polansky
*I Can Achieve Anything* by MoNique Waters
*I Want to Be a Lot* by Ashley Savage

*The Magic of Wonder* by Jenna Copper, Ashley Bible, Abby Gross, and Staci Lamb
*Micah's Big Question* by Naomi O'Brien
*The Princes of Serendip* by Allyson Apsey
*Ride with Emilio* by Richard Nares
*A Teacher's Top Secret Confidential* by LaNesha Tabb
*A Teacher's Top Secret: Mission Accomplished* by LaNesha Tabb
*The Wild Card Kids* by Hope and Wade King
*Zom-Be a Design Thinker* by Amanda Fox

www.ingramcontent.com/pod-product-compliance
Lightning Source LLC
Chambersburg PA
CBHW050553160426
43199CB00015B/2646